I Like Being Old

Praise for *I Like Being Old*

Here it is, a tidy little book of 150 pages that tells how one ordinary woman who married, raised a family, had a career and kept living — then lived decades more — turned an old age of dependence into a new life — and a new attitude — of singular courage and enjoyment. Not what we think goes with the "old age" territory.

—Liz Taylor, Seattle, editor, Aging Deliberately e-Newsletter, June 2010

This book is a "must" read for the old and the near old.... With breezy humor, Eileen makes light of the pesky barriers we oldsters encounter daily.... She acknowledges how hard but necessary it is to give up what we shouldn't do or can't do—pride and independence must give way—but we must not give up what makes life still very much worth living.

—Betty Fletcher, Seattle, Judge, United States Court of Appeals for the Ninth Circuit

I think what I admire the most in reading the book is the way Eileen looks at herself as a work in progress that she continues to shape and reinvent as she goes.... This way, living continues to be something one does out of love for the project, and she will continue to love it as long as she is alive.

—Phyllis Roberts, Mount Vernon, WA

I am now a retired seventy-two year old woman who has worked in the geriatric field for about 16 years. This is the best book I have read about aging...with grace....courage... and strength. Not strength as we value it but the inner strength which in the end of our days we can only count on.

—Mary Beth MacCauley, Vashon, WA

[A] book full of wisdom.

—Jerry Large, Columnist for the *Seattle Times*

Eileen has become a vivid personality for me....She personifies "flexibility in the face of change," the key to successful aging according to the chief researcher at the aging study where I once worked. I wish ... that many others might read [the book's] wonderfully clear and direct presentation of Eileen, her struggles, and her successes.

—Walter Eden, Seattle, WA

Socrates advised us that the "unexamined life is not worth living," and Eileen's book illustrates the point to perfection. Her close look at life and what she is doing and what she has done with life is inspiring....I've read my share of books over the years, but this book does more for me at the moment than any I can recall.

—Del Lowery, Bellingham, WA,
"Retirement Talk" podcast

I Like Being Old

A Guide to Making the Most of Aging

K. Eileen Allen
In collaboration with Judith R. Starbuck

iUniverse, Inc.
Bloomington

I Like Being Old

A Guide to Making the Most of Aging

iUniverse books may be ordered through booksellers or by contacting:
iUniverse
1663 Liberty Drive
Bloomington, IN 47403
www.iuniverse.com
1-800-Authors (1-800-288-4677)

ISBN: 978-1-936236-67-1 (pbk)
ISBN: 978-1-936236-68-8 (ebk)

Library of Congress Control Number: 2011906671

Printed in the United States of America
iUniverse rev. date: 5/23/2011

Contents

Section Two

How can I survive without my car, my own home, my independence?

Section Three
How can slowing down in old age be such a plus?

Introduction

"How come you're having such a happy, lively old age at ninety, when you can hardly see or hear?" I've heard this question more and more in the past few years, even from people who scarcely know me. And my friends have said, "You're a writer; you ought to write about your experience." So I have.

Actually, a book about good old age had been simmering on the back burner of my mind since I was in my early sixties. At that time I spent a year as a congressional science fellow on Capitol Hill in Washington DC, where I was involved with the Select Committee on Aging. That's when I started to look beyond my professional focus on child development to old age development. But the book would have been purely theoretical had I written it then.

Now I can write that book from my own experience, with not only the typical challenges of old age, but with the added challenges of severely limited vision and hearing and decreasing mobility.

Back when I turned sixty, I began thinking about the fact that I, too, was approaching old age. I began looking at old people around me, and I realized they handled aging in many different ways. On one end of the spectrum were the grumpies, who walked around with heads down, a dour expression on their faces, and complaints on their lips. In the middle were the coasters, getting old instead of growing old, not seeing options that would give them more rewarding lives. On the other end were the seekers, those who met you with a smile, were engaged in life, and were obviously having a good time.

I decided back then I wanted to be a seeker.

I finally decided in my early eighties that I should do this book. But I didn't get started until after I'd lost most of my eyesight and couldn't do it alone. So it just kept simmering … until all the pieces fell into place.

Judith Starbuck and I had been working together for several years as editors on *The Crone Connection,* a newsletter focused on women and aging. All along I'd been talking with her about this book I wanted to write. The more I talked about it, the more interested she became in working on it with me. The more interested she became, the more enthusiastic I became about our doing it together. We decided to go for it.

I couldn't believe my good fortune. Judith had a BA in journalism and had been writing for newsletters for almost fifty years. From our work together on *The Crone Connection,* I knew I admired her outstanding writing skills and her ability to collaborate with others.

We set up a schedule and began working. From the start, we went at it with enthusiasm. We looked forward to our Tuesday and Thursday work sessions, playing with words, clarifying my thoughts, and trying to balance wisdom and humor. It wasn't long before I was certain that Judith was, indeed, an able writer and also a skilled interviewer. When my pump went dry, Judith always managed to prime it and get us going again. And when I'd get discouraged or too serious, she'd remind me, "We're doing this because it's fun!"

My working with almost no vision was a tremendous challenge for both of us, but we found a system that worked. I would do what I called spewing, a fast-flowing, stream-of-consciousness way of getting words on paper. Judith would take home many pages of notes and come back with the best of my spewing, arranged in a cohesive way. She was doing the kind of editing I would have done had I been able to see. I would marvel at her incisiveness and her ability to distill my main themes and maintain my words, in my voice.

When I'd tell people I was writing a book, they'd ask me how I could do that when I couldn't see. Well, the answer is: this book would never have happened without Judith. And she tells me she got as much from our collaboration as she gave to it, finding many things which applied to her own life. She herself is on the threshold of old age at sixty-seven and is helping her ninety-one-year-old mother maintain the highest possible quality of life.

What would I like readers to get from this book? I hope my experience will show that there are surprisingly rewarding options when it comes to the obvious hurdles of old age, such as giving up driving, having to move, losing independence, and slowing down.

But more than that, I hope readers will come away with the belief that having a good old age doesn't just happen. It's up to each of us to make it happen. It's our resolve and engagement that will make old age rewarding and fun, a time to stay open to all life has to offer, an opportunity to keep learning from what comes our way.

In my own learning to get along with minimal sight, hearing, and mobility, I've discovered so much about myself. Doors have opened to show me my own personal strengths in dealing with what could be thought of as devastating change. I've also found I like being a bit adventurous, even reckless, limited as the options may be. I've found I like trying new things. So what if I flunk? It doesn't matter. I can try again and again if need be. Or I'll start looking around, because I've learned that another chance to live lively will present itself.

I really like myself for trying things I thought I couldn't do. I like the person I'm becoming as I age. Now when I look in the mirror (even though I can't really see myself), I love being able to say, "You're okay, Old Girl!" And I give myself a big smile.

So, for anyone on the aging track, from forty to one hundred and four, I hope this book will inspire you to make choices about how you grow old, and help you realize that you don't have to leave such an important matter to chance.

Section One

How can I be so happy with all the challenges I face?

Setting the Scene: The Beach

Eileen and I are sitting on a weathered bench overlooking the water in a secluded cove. The waves come in rhythmically, lapping against the bottom of the commanding rock, which will be entirely under water at high tide. During the day, gulls and herons prowl the water's edge hunting for fish, and eagles call as they circle above or perch in a fir farther down, where the bluff rises to one hundred feet. Off to our right are beds of heather, rhododendrons, juniper, and other shrubs and flowers Eileen has planted. Beyond that, across the inlet, the mountains are a majestic presence, sometimes revealed, sometimes hidden in clouds.

Rhythmic tide. Prowling birds. Heather with mountain backdrop. This bench that catches the latest sun and allows for long sitting and dreaming. The simple cabin with its crackling fire and window seat looking out at the evening light. These give sustenance almost as vital as food and sleep to Eileen.

Tonight our attention is fixed on the glow behind the madrona trees on the bluff. We're waiting for the full moon to show itself, sharing an old shawl in front of a small fire in a pit near the beach. We're talking quietly about what this isolated retreat offers Eileen, even though she can no longer do the strenuous walking, gardening, and entertaining she's enjoyed over the thirty-five years she's owned it. She mentions solitude, natural beauty, and the lack of pressure. We marvel yet again at the unexpected depth of our friendship at this time in our lives.

The moon edges above the trees. I describe it, and Eileen is able to catch a fleeting glimpse of it in the peripheral vision she still has. Eileen's delight couldn't be more genuine. Her ability to experience joy and daily happiness seems only to have intensified as her vision, hearing, and mobility have diminished. She's done more than accept her changed reality. She could easily focus on the fact that she can barely see the moon. Instead she lets the happiness of the moment flood her being.

Judith Starbuck

Chapter One

Aging in the Affirmative

I like being old!

It amazes me that I can say this, but it's true. I like having time I never felt I had before—to ponder, to muse, to feel grateful for life's many gifts. I like learning to appreciate myself more, and others too, even with our multiple warts and corns. And I have to admit it strokes my ego when I get applause from young and old for being such a lively, engaged, happy old woman.

Why do I feel this way? Old age has such a bum rap. Poor self-image, negative stereotypes, and losses of all kinds—I've had my share. But, somehow, these common challenges became incentives, rather than hindrances, for me. I thought if I worked hard enough I could keep them from getting me down.

It turns out I was right, and here I am at ninety, climbing with my high-tech knee joints onto a soapbox (with handrails of course) to say so.

Early Choices

Looking back, I realize that I've made many choices throughout my life that set me up to enjoy being old. One of the first was brought about by these very knees, long before they became high tech. I was dealing with increasing arthritis pain in my early sixties. I'd always loved walking—three to four miles at a brisk pace was the way I got around every day. Now my doctor said I had to cut way back on this kind of weight-bearing exercise.

He suggested swimming instead. I considered this ... and I balked. What about my hair? How could I bring myself to appear at a public pool in a bathing suit? How could I face going out at 5:45 in the morning, the only time I could find in my busy life? Also, it had been years since I'd done any swimming. Even way back then, I could only take as many strokes as one breath lasted, then would have to stand up and pant before going on. But I decided to try.

My second time in the pool, floundering about, sputtering and grasping at the edges, I noticed one of my graduate students watching me. When I told him I was trying to learn to swim all over again, he hesitantly asked if I'd like some help. (Graduate students are naturally cautious about approaching their professors this way.)

"Oh, I would love it!" I gasped. We met several times at the pool, and he coached me to coordinate my breathing and arms and legs so I didn't look like a disjointed lobster trying to get through the water. Once I got my body parts organized and into sync it became easier and easier. After several months I was swimming a nonstop crawl for forty-five minutes every weekday morning. I couldn't believe I was doing this. (It's funny how well my graduate student did that year.)

Thus began years of serious swimming. The payoff was increased flexibility and the sense of well-being I'd felt before from walking.

Taking up swimming turned out to be the first of many adaptations. Over the next few decades, I had to literally reinvent myself when faced with hearing loss, near blindness, and decreasing mobility. I sometimes congratulate myself that I was able to face these challenges head-on rather than denying them or giving up.

Focusing on What I Can Do

True enough, this old girl ain't what she used to be. Lucky me that it doesn't take good looks, good health, or a good memory to be able to proclaim, "I like being old!" Contrary to what many others are reporting, my life seems to be getting better instead of worse. I seem to find increasing satisfaction in focusing on what I can do rather than on what I can't do.

Actually, this was a principle I learned early in my research on child development: start with what the child can do, and build on that, step by step. Now I'm applying this to myself in old age. I know this step-by-step strategy is helping me face challenges and make adaptations.

Good Advice

I'll never forget the night my longtime friend Betty and I closed down a restaurant at 2:00 AM, discussing, of all things, happiness. She introduced me to the concept that each of us is the author of our own happiness. I had to ponder this for a long time before I could truly believe that whether I'm happy or not is up to me. I gradually realized if

I really want to be happy, nobody can stop me. Conversely, nobody else can make me happy.

When I was in my early seventies, I encountered "the discipline of gratitude" when I heard about a commencement address Hillary Clinton had given on that topic. This struck a chord. It has led me to the practice of consciously acknowledging the things that bring me joy. My life is enriched each time I tune in to the pleasure of a hot shower, basking in the sun, an engaging conversation, doing work I enjoy, or just sitting.

Another benchmark in attitude change came when I heard about Raymond Carver, a well-known Northwest poet, as he was dying. When asked, "Did you get what you wanted out of life?" he replied, "I did."

"And what was that?" His answer: "To call myself beloved." By this time into my seventies, I discovered I too wanted to go out liking and respecting myself. I began to assess what was good about me. I decided then that somehow I would learn to "call myself beloved." I'm still working on that, but I've made progress.

Also in my midseventies, I was exposed for the first time to the idea that women in their sixties, seventies, and eighties could make good lives for themselves. My husband of more than fifty years had just died, and I was living alone for the first time in my life. A friend introduced me to Crone, a local older women's group. When I discovered its mission was to help women grow old "with power, passion, and purpose," I knew right away I wanted to be part of it. Many Crones, like me, had already lost a spouse and some of the capabilities of their younger years. These women proved to be powerful models for the new role I was taking on. Now I am told that I, in my turn, have become a model for others.

I've Discovered ...

When I was in my seventies, I realized that I could keep learning. Contrary to popular belief, the brain does not quit on us when we get old. It keeps working as long as we keep using it. Research seems to show that if we keep trying, new pathways in the brain may be created to compensate for capabilities we have lost.

I'm watching in my own life as my body and its systems almost miraculously realign themselves to help me adapt to physical changes. For example, I have a heightened awareness of what's going on around me—where things are, when someone comes into the room—which has helped me adjust to my loss of vision. And I've developed an ability to memorize poetry since I've had to give up reading. This amazes me. The key appears to be to keep going, keep that brain working. I'm so grateful I do still have that capacity.

Change Is Inevitable

Change is inevitable, and I've had to face my share of it. At different stages I wondered how I could live without driving a car, how I could possibly give up the home I loved, how this fiercely independent woman could accept the help she increasingly needed. I've had to adjust to all of these now. The consequences weren't so disastrous after all. On the contrary, there were times I came upon unexpected rewards. I wouldn't have predicted that giving up driving would lead to new friendships and some creative ways of weaning myself from car dependency.

This brings me to options. I see many more possibilities now than I used to. It's like I've taken the blinders off and opened up to what's always been there. It's important to keep reminding myself that whenever I'm cut off from what worked for me in the past, I need to start looking around for other possibilities. That's how, when I had to give up reading, I found not only poetry but several new friends who read to me—which turned out to be a rich experience for all involved.

Instead of sitting on the pity pot, I've found that taking responsibility for my own well-being is a better way to make life work. My single-parent mother and I had almost nothing during my childhood. But almost as bad as the poverty was the fact that there was not one book in the house. There was not the slightest thought that I would go to college. I hear people say their childhoods ruined their lives. My experience is the opposite. Instead of scarring me, this background seems to have taught me to live with what I have, roll with the punches, and take advantage of opportunities when they arise.

But more about all of these—happiness, change, options, unexpected rewards—in the chapters to come.

Pondering

Where, I've often wondered, did my strength to move beyond my limited background come from? Maybe a hardscrabble life develops strength. Maybe I wouldn't be the kind of old woman I am today if I hadn't had to overcome so much. I guess I must have had some innate smarts that made me start reading voraciously as soon as books were available to me around the age of five. It seems that I may have been given more than my share of determination to go on to become a university professor after not having started college until I was in my midthirties.

Now that I'm old, it's a marvel to me that I can incorporate my more recent disabilities into a good life. Could it be my nature to turn hardship to strength instead of defeat? Maybe it's partly my age. At this stage of life I realize I can try new things and take risks I wouldn't have thought possible when I was younger and afraid to make mistakes.

But these successes didn't come easily. I've worked hard at having a good old age. I've reaped the benefits of earlier choices, even though I'm only now recognizing their significance. One thing I know for sure: It's never too late to learn and to change. I plan to be learning and changing until the curtain falls. And I expect to enjoy being old until that day.

Chapter Two

Taking on Challenges

I can't see much. I can't hear much. I can't walk much.

I've come to think of my almost total blindness, serious hearing loss, and need for a cane or walker as "challenges" instead of handicaps. This makes me feel I can do something about them.

In contrast, earlier labels—handicapped, disabled, impaired, and even crippled—had the opposite effect. Too often they led to hopelessness and a negative self-image. I've decided I'm not going to buy that hopelessness or that negative image.

But it's been difficult. Reading, writing, and vigorous walking were the things I'd always considered the most important for a full life. And now they're gone! However, it doesn't do any good to dwell on "why has this happened to me?" Instead I'm learning to say, "So be it." My limitations are here to stay. I have to find a way to live with them. I say to myself, "I will have a good old age in spite of them!"

Early Losses

My challenges started in my early sixties. I began to wake up to the possibility of hearing loss. Could it be that my friends and students were actually speaking up? Could it be that their "mumbling" was my problem—I wasn't hearing? My denial ended when the audiologist reported I was hearing only about 50 percent of what was going on. So that began a now-twenty-five-year relationship with hearing aids, and it hasn't been easy.

By then I was already plagued by arthritis. At times I've been severely challenged by the pain, at other times exasperated by near immobility. Over the years I've become more and more limited and have had to come up with new ways of managing.

My third challenge, and probably the most stressful, is loss of vision due to macular degeneration. I am legally blind. I can't drive or shop on my own. I can't read, regardless of the size of the type, not even notes I write to myself. It's no longer possible to use a computer for e-mail or to explore the Net. I don't see the face of anyone I encounter and wonder if I'd even recognize myself if I met me on the street!

I do have some health conditions not uncommon in my age group: atrial fibrillation, congestive heart failure, sleep apnea, and some incontinence. But, at this point, these conditions don't have as much impact on my daily life as the hearing, mobility, and vision losses. So I'm going to discuss these three main challenges in more detail.

— *Hearing* —

It's been a long time since I could hear the morning chorus of birds I love. Just about the only bird I can still hear is the raucous great blue heron, and, believe me, I'm grateful to hear that. But, more important, my hearing loss is making communication increasingly frustrating. Essentially, I'm not nearly as active a participant in groups as I used to be. I miss so much of the discussion going on around me. This becomes an issue more often now that I eat some of my meals in a large dining room. Generally speaking, people have to say things to me two, three, and four times, and sometimes I never do get what they say.

That means it's not only hard for me, but it's hard for those who have to deal with me.

Over and over I hear how annoyed others get when those of us with deafness don't wear our hearing aids. I got my first set of hearing aids when I was sixty-two. Right from the start, I couldn't seem to adjust to them. Yes, I did hear better part of the time, but so much of the time they bothered me. My ears itched. I couldn't stand listening to myself chew. My feet made such a lot of noise on the carpet. Restaurants and other public places overwhelmed me; it seemed like every sound was magnified.

This was in spite of "state-of-the-art" hearing aids that are supposed to screen out extraneous noise. I wasn't able to fully adapt to any of the five sets I got over twenty-five years. And there isn't anything unusual about my hearing loss. It is severe, but it has a perfectly normal, predictable pattern.

Just Wear Them

When I was getting my sixth pair, I asked the audiologist, "Why do you suppose this doesn't work for me?" I confessed I sometimes referred to myself as "the recalcitrant hearing aid wearer." Then, all of a sudden, the answer to my own question came to me: "I wonder if I'm not doing my part?"

Right then I decided to take responsibility for learning to use these expensive, state-of-the art gadgets I was getting.

In retrospect, it appears that my main problem was ignoring clinicians' advice. I didn't wear my hearing aids all the time because they bothered me so much. Up until a few years ago, I only put them in when I was with people. And I've lived alone for the last fifteen years, so they weren't in my ears much of the time.

According to the audiologist, this put my brain in a real dilemma, never getting a chance to adapt to the amplification, because the hearing aids were sometimes in, sometimes not. So I have been working on myself to put the hearing aids in as soon as I've had my shower in the morning and wear them until bedtime. My diligence hasn't produced a miracle cure, but I'm doing much better. This experience has brought home to me the principle that whatever problem I encounter, I'd better look first for the answer in myself.

— *Mobility* —

Walking has always been my joy, my therapy, my time for creative cogitation. Way back, when my walking was becoming a bit unsteady—my, how I resisted even carrying a cane! Then, several years later, it became obvious I needed more support than the cane I'd finally adjusted to. Again I resisted, but I got my walker in my early eighties after a dramatic wake-up call.

I tripped in the street when I was out walking and fell flat on my face. My cane flew out of reach. "How am I going to get up?" I asked myself. I spied the post of a stop sign about four feet away and dragged myself to it on my stomach. There I pulled myself up to my knees. On my knees, I made my way to my cane and back to the post again. Then I could stand up. But I realized how lucky I was that this was a little-traveled street.

I found I was not seriously injured, though my pride had suffered a terrible blow. But the important lesson was: if I'd had a walker I'd have saved myself the ignominy, and especially the peril, of a bad fall. I went home and immediately called my friend who'd been urging me to get a walker. "Can we go walker shopping," I asked, "today, I hope?" Mission accomplished that very day.

Now I love my walker. I almost never leave home without it. Now I never think of it as stigmatizing, the main reason I didn't use it in the first place. I no longer feel it advertises to the world that I'm old and don't function very well. On the contrary, it has enhanced my functioning. I'm safer, and I feel so much more competent with it. I walk more briskly. It frees me to be more aware of what's going on around me.

I'm so grateful every time I use it that Medicare and I could afford to buy a really good one.

In Praise of My Walker

It is a great walker! It's lightweight and highly maneuverable. It folds up. It has a handy seat, so if I get tired, I can put the brakes on, pull the seat down, and be as comfortable as can be. It has a nice basket for my purse and the leaves, stones, and cones I'm likely to pick up. It's a pretty, shiny dark red. I get so many questions from people who want to know where to get one for someone they know that I think I should carry the manufacturer's cards.

At holiday time, several of us in our building decorated our walkers. One resident got battery-operated lights when she took her walker on the luminary walk around the lake. I resolved to get some of these for next year. But its great features and beauty are not the only advantages. I can go so much faster with my walker. Not that I'm any speed demon, but striding along with it, I feel like I'm actually getting some exercise. I look forward to getting out for a walk now almost as much as when I could do it on my own. I'm determined to defy the image of the oldster hunched over, gripping the handles as if on a runaway horse. When I make a point of standing upright and moving freely, I even feel younger.

— *Vision* —

Losing my vision to macular degeneration has been a real blow. Reading, writing, enjoying natural beauty, and taking care of myself seemed essential to my good quality of life. But now I have to wait to read the new books everyone's talking about until they come out in recorded version. I can't see the intricacies of my favorite flowers or the faces of friends; nobody ages, including myself, because I can't see the wrinkles and gray hair. I can't drive to the store to get my own groceries. And once I get there, I can't pick out what I want. I'm liable to come home with eggnog instead of two-percent milk. And I do miss the Scrabble, cribbage, and bridge that provided light-hearted competitive fun with friends.

Getting through a typical day is a series of major and minor frustrations. I can't see to pick up the pieces of the wineglass I've knocked over, can't read labels on the cans in my cupboard, and can't find the papers that seem always to have perversely misplaced themselves. I even have to wait to see what's in the mail until someone comes who can tell me.

My table manners leave much to be desired. There's a ring of errant food around my plate after most meals. I spill things. I find myself more and more often picking up a chicken leg or a piece of beef in the stew with my fingers or shoveling the peas onto a fork with a forefinger.

I ask myself which is worse: the mess or using my fingers. I try to pretend I'm not embarrassed. I look around covertly to see if anyone is watching. But my tablemates assure me that it's okay, that I'm doing fine. I have to accept the fact that I'm never going to win any table manners awards. I have to say, "So be it."

I'd Rather Do It Myself!

But I'm putting off as long as possible having someone else cut up my food and put it in my mouth. I'm even getting a kick out of the role reversal when one or the other of my sons, with a wicked gleam in his eye, pretends to spit on his napkin to clean up my face.

I want to do for myself as much as I can. I rely a lot on touch now. I feel my earrings by outline, my clothes by fabric, and my medicine bottles by shape. I group my earrings (silver and gold), my clothes (blouses, jackets, pants), and my accessories (gloves, hats, scarves) to make identification easier.

Though I have no central vision, I have enough peripheral vision to get around in familiar places, often alone, always with a cane or my walker for safety. I don't venture out even for short walks without one of these, because both lack of vision and loss of balance make me quite unsteady. If I have a friendly arm to take, I choose one of my favorite canes. If I'm going on my own where others need to identify me as blind, I take my distinctive white cane.

Lost!

Sometimes even a cane isn't enough. I remember all too vividly the time several years ago when I was staying at my son's house in another city. I decided to go for a walk on my own. I enjoyed myself for several blocks, but soon I noticed that there were no straight streets, and, of course, I couldn't read street signs. I decided I'd better go back before I got lost.

But it was too late! I was already lost. After many wrong turns, I was getting close to panic. A young man was waiting at a bus stop and asked if he could help. I couldn't even remember my son's address, but I could remember his phone number. The young man whipped out his cell phone and called my son, who a few minutes later came striding along to retrieve his lost mother.

... and Found

I'm so grateful for the help I've received from a therapist from Community Services for the Blind and Partially Sighted (CSBPS). She taught me strategies for crossing streets more safely and stressed the importance of wearing very light-colored clothes to make me more visible. But she also pointed out a couple of intersections where under no circumstances should I attempt to cross alone, period.

She also taught me the miracle of Velcro. When I was still using a stove, little strips marked Off and 350 on the oven dial. And all the gadgets I try to use, like the tape player and TV remote, have those little strips marking the On button.

This helper also stressed the old adage my mother raised me on: "A place for everything and everything in its place." She pointed out that if I put something down carelessly, it could lead to a half-hour search. How well I know the truth of that! One time my hearing aid ended up on a salad plate on the second shelf of the cupboard, where a friend found it three weeks after I'd lost it. How it got there will remain a mystery. When I do put things in their places instead of hither, thither, and yon, it's often possible to avoid such frustrations.

Would you believe it?—all these valuable CSBPS services are free!

Surprising Benefits

Sometimes it's necessary to rely on the kindness of strangers. And the miracle is that again and again someone will cheerfully respond to my requests. They might be in the checkout line just ahead of or behind me and hear me ask for help to get through a busy intersection outside. It's such a relief to hear, "I have time; let me help you across the street."

I remember the young skateboarder who saw me struggling to get up a hill and asked if he could help. "Yes, you certainly can!" I gasped. After he'd parked his skateboard, he matched my pace, pulling my walker while I pushed, and between us we got me topside. Each of us went our own way. What a lovely experience it was.

It is really heartwarming to have these encounters, and I do have a lot of them, in all kinds of situations. I know it's hard to believe, and it may make me sound like a Pollyanna, but this kind of experience truly is one of the many positive side effects of these challenges I live with every day.

A sense of humor is often needed to see the positive. Judith and I were taking a spring walk in a beautiful remnant of old-growth forest in one of the city parks. I called Judith over to look at a snowy-white trillium flower I'd spied by the side of the path. I'm glad I could laugh when she said, "Eileen, I'm afraid that's sun-whitened dog do."

Pondering

There are a few common threads running through my adaptations to the challenges I face. One is overcoming my own initial resistance. I didn't want the stigma of being seen as old because I was using hearing aids, a cane, or a walker. But in all these cases, accepting the inevitable—that I need them to live well with new realities—lets these devices give me a much higher quality of life.

A second thread is acceptance. I have to accept my limitations. There's no going back. It's up to me to make the best of what I have. Sometimes it's better to take the easy way when the alternatives are just too hard. For instance, I keep my radio on my two favorite stations because I can't tune it. I find I can get along okay with that.

I also have to accept lots of help. Some people are going to help willingly and patiently, while others will find my limitations frustrating and hard to deal with. It's my job to keep tuned in to the signs people give about how they're reacting and to adjust accordingly.

Third, I need to take stock frequently, making a realistic assessment of my current abilities and of the dangers I may face. Being less capable means I have to take more responsibility for my own safety.

One more thing I have to do is to keep trying to use my remaining vision, hearing, and mobility so my brain has a chance to adapt and compensate. This has truly paid off for me. Sometimes it seems that I have extrasensory perception when I "see" something I know can't be coming through my damaged eyes.

I'm amazed that I don't feel weighed down by these daily difficulties. Instead, I seem to enjoy the problem solving it takes to keep these challenges from limiting me even further. And I keep coming back to the fact that, even with the loss of so much I used to consider essential, I can continue to be so much in love with life.

Chapter Three

Choosing to Be Happy

Happiness is an inside job.

I am happy, and I know it. But why is this? Friends and family have been asking for years, "How do you do it, when you can hardly see, hear, or walk?" It's taken a long time to come to the place where I can proclaim: "It's up to me. I choose to be happy."

Learning to Be Happy

Certainly I can't say I've been happy all my life.

I remember when I was about ten years into my role as a young wife and mother, I told my family physician that I felt my husband and I weren't making each other happy. His counsel was: "Eileen, nobody can make another person happy. Happiness needs to come from within each of us." Since I didn't seem to know how to implement this, I just kept muddling along.

Later on, my older son, with the irreverence of a young teenager, gave me some advice. Using his pet name for his early-graying mother, he said, "Moldylocks, lighten up!" I sputtered, "But … but, there's so much to do, so little time, so little money." But the message did penetrate, and every now and then I heard his words in my head.

Then, as I mentioned earlier, when I was about forty-five, I was talking about being happy with my best friend, Betty. She had a strong philosophical bent. She stated, "It is the responsibility of each of us to be happy." When I asked her what she meant, in a nutshell, her reply was, "Here we are, most of us with all of the essentials for a good life, and we need to honor this bounty by being happy." Unchurched as she was, she went on to say she even thought it was "a sin" not to be happy with all we had.

This notion of personal responsibility reinforced my doctor's statement of twenty years earlier. It gave me something to chew on—and chew on it I did. That one word kept prodding me: responsibility. It was a mandate, the way she put it. Basically, I had to agree with her.

What else did I need? I had children who were growing up to be good students and good citizens, a husband who had been a good partner all through the years, a nice home, and work that I loved. It was true, I was giving a great deal of myself to maintain these aspects of my life, and my stress level and energy output were extremely high. But this didn't take away from the bounty I had.

I began to get glimmerings that it was the stuff of everyday life that made up what I thought of as happiness. Stresses continued, but I began to acknowledge more consciously—at least part of the time—all the good in my life.

Putting on a Happy Face

What came next was a practical application. I took a position at the University of Kansas when my husband retired and was willing to come with me. Within two months of joining the faculty, I felt I'd made the worst mistake of my life. The only thing I could see to do was resign. It seemed to me the faculty and students didn't like me and considered me an intruder. I hadn't recognized my responsibility in setting up this situation. My attitude toward the program—that it wasn't up to my standards—communicated itself to the people I was supposed to work with. I was creating the climate for what appeared to be their aloofness and nonacceptance.

Then a longtime friend, whose advice I'd trusted for many years, stepped into the picture. He told me, "You can't resign until you've solved the problem of why this isn't working. You can't resign while you're down."

"What'll I do?" I wailed.

"You're a smart woman," he pointed out to me. "You'll figure it out."

So I tried. The first decision I made was that I needed to act cheerful, though I was perfectly miserable. I put my son's advice of years before to work and tried to lighten up. Now when I met a colleague in the hall or in a meeting, I pasted a smile on my face and said a few cheery words, inane as I felt they were and as fake as I felt the smile was.

But the atmosphere did seem to be changing, so I began employing similar tactics with my students. Again the atmosphere changed, little by little. And so did my attitude. The pasted-on smile and the inane pleasantries began to be genuine. And, amazingly enough, my evaluation of the program also began to change. I came to see that what I'd thought were weaknesses were simply differences, even strengths. When I started to do things "their" way, it didn't take long to see that my way wasn't necessarily better.

I'm the Author of My Own Happiness

The upshot of this story was that by the end of that school year I had found my niche. I was thoroughly enjoying my job, my colleagues, and my students and was even rejoicing that I had made the change. In other words, I was happy! I'd demonstrated to myself that I could be the author of my own happiness. Ever since, I've been applying my belief that I can make daily choices to stay happy. Every success confirms it.

Old age has added challenges, however. Now happiness often seems harder to come by. As we age, my friends and I seem to be losing much of what we have assumed makes us happy—material things, travel, an active life, recognition.

I've had to look for happiness in different places. Sometimes before I go to sleep at night, I consciously acknowledge some of the things that made me happy that day. They tend to be as simple as the glow from a conversation with a friend I haven't seen for years, a clutch of ducklings falling into the lake in their mother's wake, or a tune on the radio that brought up memories of courtship days. I notice the list is now made up of few momentous events and lots of treasured moments.

What Makes Me Happy Now

Most of us have some activities that make us happy: cooking a gourmet meal, listening to music, making bread from scratch, digging in the garden, playing bridge, watching Monday night football.

For me, happiness is being outdoors. I've always been a "nature girl." The more time I can spend out in the elements, even just on my little balcony, the happier I am. Walking is one of my primary joys, although I now have to do it with my walker. Living where I can go across the street and walk for ten minutes or two hours along a beautiful urban lake is a major contribution to my happiness. Of course, spending time at my beach place is also at the top of the list. I'm never happier than when I'm sitting on my weathered bench listening to the water lapping on the shore and feeling the sun and wind on my face.

Happiness is realizing that so far I haven't lost all my smarts. It makes me happy to do work that I love and feel is important. For example, at times, working on this book has flooded me with happiness. Learning poetry and listening to good books often do the same. It makes me happy that I can still have lively conversations, still deliver the occasional one-liner that makes people laugh, still put out good ideas that get used. It delights me that I can still have fun playing with words and numbers and, when I'm at the store, make change in my head quickly.

Happiness is finding the balance between reaching out to people and spending time with myself. It's new for me to strike up conversations with people I meet casually. I'm finding this rewarding with the upbeat people in my retirement center as well as with the strangers I meet while out walking. At the same time, I continue to treasure the love, the acceptance, and the depth of sharing that my long-term friendships provide. And I never come away from a service or coffee hour at my Unitarian-Universalist church without feeling excited about my conversations with people who share my values.

On the other end of the balance scale is spending time alone, in my apartment or at my beach place. Solitude offers the pleasure of really getting to know myself. At the beach, life is pared down to the essentials—food, a fire, the wind, and the waves. In my apartment, I delight in my own space in the midst of this huge complex. Everything is familiar, just the way I want it. I'm constantly amazed at how much joy I get from my own company, where I can think my own thoughts and don't feel pulled a hundred ways.

Happiness is getting rid of the "oughts." I no longer feel I'm bound by other people's ideas of how I should live my life or even by what I thought I "had to do" earlier in my life. I'm glad I no longer have all the obligations—the many board meetings, the committee meetings. This leaves me time to practice my meditation, learn a new poem, or go out for a walk.

Last, but certainly not least, happiness is my family. It's following my great-grandson's development through the loving eyes of his grandmother, my daughter. It's listening to my sons' laughter as they work together to clear brush at my beach place. It's family gatherings where Mom/Grandma/G-Ma/Aunt Eileen has such a special place as the matriarch. I'm proud to be a part of this production, this theater piece that is my family, where the main supporting characters, my children, are already senior citizens.

I'm Grateful to Be Me

As I think about how happy I am with these various parts of my life, I also notice I've come to be happier with myself, to trust myself more, to appreciate myself more. In other words, I'm quite happy being me. And I'm grateful to be aware I'm happy. I mentioned earlier my response to Hillary Clinton's "discipline of gratitude." Gratitude is tightly interwoven with my happiness.

How is gratitude different from "counting one's blessings"? It's more than a mere listing of all the good things in my life. It's allowing feelings to well up, paying attention when something touches my heart.

A dazzling sunrise offers its glory for only a few moments, and I miss the joy it brings if I don't acknowledge it right then and there. I want to revel in the tenderness when my great grandbaby reaches out to explore my wrinkled face and thrill at my first hearing of beautifully written words. If I don't acknowledge, consciously name, and rejoice in that which rises from within moment by moment, I may never get a another chance.

The Role of Acceptance

An important ingredient of happiness is acceptance of what is. My lifelong response to challenging situations has been to fix them "right now." Nowadays this is often not possible. Increasingly, I'm able to say, "So be it! I'll wait until someone can help me." And then I look for something that's not frustrating and brings me pleasure. I may pick up the phone to chat with a friend, recite a poem, or look out the window to catch a glimpse of clouds reflected on the lake.

I seem to be learning to let go of activities I used to consider essential. And amazingly, instead of making me sad, this makes me happy. As I write this, I think about the conference I didn't attend. How happy I am not to have to do all the planning and packing. Instead, I can stay home to do the things that now mean more to me.

Pondering

Now, again, I don't want to sound like a Pollyanna. Of course things go wrong and make me unhappy. But long ago, when I pasted the smile on my face in Kansas, I learned a powerful lesson: Wallowing in discontent doesn't help a bit—and neither does feeling like a victim. I have to keep remembering I'm the one, the only one, who has to shape up and focus on what makes me happy.

Especially in my old age, when I start feeling like a victim, despairing over losses and changes, I remind myself that the way to get off the pity pot is to take to heart this quote I had on my refrigerator for years: "If you really want to be happy, no one can stop you."

I no longer believe every cloud has a silver lining, but my ninety years have taught me there are always options, always alternatives, always other paths. I may not have control over circumstances, but I do have control over my own attitude and my responses. I always have the option to tune in to the little song sparrow singing outside.

I think the key is knowing and believing I can choose happiness. It's my decision.

My younger son scratched a quote on a piece of driftwood on my eighty-third birthday: "True happiness lies not in having what you want, but in wanting what you have." This has become a guiding principle in my old age. I've come to the place where I recognize I have all I want, all I need. This awareness is all it takes to prove to me that happiness is indeed an inside job.

Chapter Four

Reinventing Myself

Old age has forced me to reinvent myself.

A women's group, a walker, poetry—I've brought these things into my life to help me adapt to changes as I've aged. They're part of my strategy to do everything in my power to ensure a healthy, happy old age.

Reinventing oneself isn't easy, partly because it involves change. Change is threatening to all of us. It's hard to stop defending the way things have been. I don't want to deny my past—it's the stuff my life is made of. But it's time to shift my gaze forward. Now I need to recognize my strengths and keep looking beyond my limitations. Finding new activities and attitudes to replace ones that no longer work is surely paying off for me.

In the Company of Old Women

One of the most important ways I've gone about reinventing myself is by getting involved in Crone, the older women's group I mentioned earlier. It encourages "personal unfolding and passage … from past outgrown roles and stereotypes into powerful, passionate, and satisfying old womanhood."

I discovered in Crone the pleasure of women's groups, which had never been especially appealing to me. This can-do bunch of women exposed me to a variety of ways to start over in old age.

Phyllis took up painting when she was approaching eighty. She learned from a how-to series on television and caught fire. She found it a satisfying replacement for photography in the mountains, where she could no longer hike. Peggy took an African drumming class for seniors and welcomed this new passion into her life. She helped form a fiery group called Crone Thunder, which performed frequently around town. She even used this vigorous activity to speed her recovery from a mastectomy.

Carol loved shopping and needed a little extra income. So she prowled thrift stores and bought things she couldn't resist, then stitched some of the items together to make wearable art. The rest she resold at weekly parking-lot sales. Christina loved animals. She supplemented her limited income by dog-sitting. She also volunteered as a docent at the zoo. She turned both into ways to keep active and involved.

What a Difference a Walker Makes

The threat of change breeds resistance, and I'm no exception.

As I said earlier, I resisted getting a walker for a long time, because I felt it was a badge of old age. But now I wouldn't consider living without it. Before the walker, I resisted using a cane. I finally had to give in because of increasing arthritis. In its turn, the cane gave me greater freedom and protection.

When I had to give up reading, I thought the world as I knew it would surely come to an end. Books had been my passion from the moment I learned to read. I never could get enough of reading, and I couldn't imagine living without it. Yes, I know, talking books and all kinds of fascinating tapes and CDs are available. Thank heavens for these resources. I don't know what I'd do without them. They go a long way toward replacing the printed word, even with the intrusion of the reader's voice. But for me, and many like me, it simply is not the same as curling up with a book anywhere, anytime, holding it in my hands, turning the pages, and immersing myself.

Poetry, Anyone?

Finding a replacement for reading involved several steps. One step was learning about poetry. The leader of a group at my church recited poetry at the drop of a hat. I told him during a break one night how much I admired his ability. I said I'd never been able to understand poetry and knew I couldn't learn to recite it.

He said I could. I said I couldn't. He said he knew I could. I said I knew I couldn't. He said, "you can" and turned away to call the group back to order. I was pretty sure I couldn't, but I decided I would prove I was right.

Three weeks later I'd proved him right. I'd learned a Sarah Teasdale poem about the sea, and I was so pleased with myself that I recited it for the group. Not only did I thoroughly enjoy myself, but I wowed them! So I decided to try another. Before long I was learning and reciting lots of poems and starting to love poetry.

Then, at church one day, several of us were talking about a book our minister had mentioned in his sermon.

I said if I could still read I would rush right down to the bookstore and buy it. Margaret said, "I have it. I've read it; yes, it's wonderful, and why don't I come and read it to you?" A couple of books down the road, we discovered a mutual love of poetry. She's still reading poetry to me every week—nine years later.

I never would have imagined it, but I've found poetry is filling the void created when I could no longer read. It's not the same, but it's exciting to find the distillation of concepts, philosophies, stories, and history that poetry offers. I hear the sounds of words and sentences, pass them through my own perceptions, and marvel over them in my memory. The concise and beautiful language fills the desperate need I've always had to make words a part of me.

Just Be

Never would I have predicted that meditation would help me reinvent myself in my old age. I dabbled with transcendental meditation in the 1960s and '70s, but I couldn't clear the space in my too-busy life for what I see now would have been so helpful. I dropped it and didn't think about it again until my mideighties. Then my younger son rekindled my interest by telling me about his experiences with meditation over almost thirty years. He taught me some meditation techniques and suggested I find a group to practice with. A friend steered me to what turned out to be the perfect group for me.

I had no idea what a meditation practice could do. Over three years of almost daily practice, I've come to fully appreciate the quietness, the focus, the first-time awareness of my own innate worth. We hear in many places the importance of being present in each moment. Meditation has helped me understand a little bit about what that means and how to sometimes achieve this being in the now.

While meditating, I include my gratitude for the abundance of good things I have in my life. I also spend some time focusing on attitudes I'd like to incorporate and on ways I'd like to be.

Novice that I am, I feel sure the peaceful quietness I find in meditation will keep me practicing the rest of my days.

Listening

Becoming a better listener is another way I'm trying to reinvent myself. This involves paying attention to what others are saying instead of formulating my own response while they're talking. It means reflecting on their ideas instead of jumping in with my always-ready pearls of wisdom. Often it means keeping my mouth shut, so my ears and mind can be open.

I didn't realize how much I tended to dominate conversations, often switching direction to something of interest to me, instead of allowing the speaker to follow through and letting others respond. I got a wake-up call when the facilitator in a small group told me I was intimidating. I was shocked. I couldn't be intimidating! But I began to listen to myself, to hear how I must sound to others. I decided I didn't want to be an old know-it-all.

I'm far from having cured myself, but I am working on changing. Now I'm enjoying hearing the interesting things other people have to say.

A related problem I'm working on is not so much about listening as it is about hearing. I do hear some of many conversations, but when I don't, I tend to break in when others are talking without realizing I'm doing it. I distinctly remember being very annoyed when a ninety-one-year-old friend with a serious hearing problem did this several years ago. I knew she didn't mean to be rude, but I thought she somehow ought to sense that someone else was already talking. Now, with my limited hearing, I've found myself doing the same thing!

This problem is not so easy to solve, I now realize, but I'm finding some ways. Especially in a smaller group, if I glance carefully around, I can often sense when someone is speaking. Their movements are different. And, if I really listen, I can often hear that something is being said, even when I can't hear the words. If I can balance my eagerness to get out what I want to say with attentiveness to those around me, I'll be able to continue to participate in the conversations I still enjoy.

Backtracking

One of my first experiences with reinventing myself occurred when I was a middle-aged professor, taking myself very seriously. I decided it was time to take the advice of my son, who had been telling me for years to lighten up. I didn't really know how, so I started watching people I thought were funny. Then I shamelessly copied them, but never in their presence, of course. To my surprise, people laughed, and I enjoyed the role of the performer! Little by little the humor started coming naturally. Most people who know me today are surprised when I tell them I haven't always been funny.

At age sixty-two, I was already having serious arthritis pain in my knees. As I said earlier, I took up swimming in spite of my initial resistance to giving up walking. I continued this form of exercise for forty-five minutes every weekday for the next twenty years. Something I'd thought I couldn't do, it turned out I could do. And it was valuable for both my body and my spirit.

When I could no longer drive myself to a pool, I gave up swimming, with much regret.

It's Worth a Risk

Knee joint replacement was first suggested when I was sixty-eight. I delayed and reevaluated for years, while the risk factors—hemorrhage, stroke, staph infection, heart failure, even death—kept increasing. At age eighty-five, when my limited ability to walk was having a major impact on the quality of my life, I assessed again. I had a favorable interview with a doctor I liked, but again I was stopped by the usual litany of risk factors.

Then one night, I was sitting in my apartment weighing all the risks and advantages one more time. What suddenly came to me was: "So what? I've had eighty-five good years, and if I die on the operating table, that's a quick and easy way to go. It's worth the risk." I called and made an appointment the next day. Since the surgery, the freedom to walk without pain has proved that risk well worth taking.

A Little of This, a Little of That

Here are a few other notions I'm using to enhance my old age.

I dabble. I put aside my fear of new things and give them a try. Children sample things in a hit-and-miss fashion to find out what works for them. It's the same at the other end of life. I figure I won't be able to discover what's good for me now if I'm not willing to experiment.

Even if I've tried something earlier and it didn't work then, I give it another go. I'm different now, and it may fit. If not, I can always put it aside. When we were young we were told not to be reckless, but maybe it's good to be a little reckless when we're more mature. People where I live can't believe I walk all the way around the lake—by myself—but doing so is one of my greatest joys.

Another thing I try to do is think "outside the box." Take canes, for example. When I finally realized I had to use one, a friend decorated a drugstore cane and gave it to me. It was beautiful. This gave me an idea: I could use this stick to make a fashion statement. I began a cane collection, and friends found interesting ones for me in thrift stores and in their travels. One of my favorites, though not my most beautiful or practical, is the one with the rearview mirror and Saxon horn.

For a long time I've been told I should loosen up. I'm trying to do this now by reaching out to people in ways I used to think were too forward. This opens doors I never imagined and often brings forth delightful responses. Joking with the barista in Starbucks, sharing a comical observation with a stranger on the trail, or striking up a conversation with the person in front of me in the grocery line sends me home with a smile on my face.

I'm learning about shifting gears. I no longer think I can do it all. I don't have to take responsibility for everything I'm involved in. Alas, I'm not indispensable. This letting go gives me the freedom to look at the contributions I can make and then leave the field open for others.

Pondering

Trying new things, taking risks, embracing change, shifting gears—all require letting go of a lot of assumptions we've made about ourselves. But I've learned the payoffs are enormous. They've culminated in a new and satisfying design for this stage of my life. I no longer live with the stress of having to be competitive. I'm much more comfortable with mutually agreeable and reciprocal arrangements. I'm also finding such joy in quiet and solitude and in having the leisure to look within.

I can now stand back and look at the jigsaw puzzle that represents my life, most of it already nicely pieced together over the last ninety years. I'm choosing the final pieces to complete the picture—ones that show an old woman reinventing herself as many times as it takes to stay engaged and in love with life.

Section Two

How can I survive without my car, my own home, my independence?

Setting the Scene: The Lake

A tree-lined, 2.7-mile path encircles this city jewel—Green Lake. People of all descriptions—walking, biking, pushing strollers—make it a vibrant community gathering place. Eileen learned to swim here as a skinny eight-year-old, and as an adult she walked here for years, delighting in the changes of the seasons. The lake was a big reason Eileen chose the Hearthstone retirement center as a place to live. It's right across the street!

Eileen is back to walking at the lake, rain or shine, in good Northwest rain gear, of course. She often describes to me the interesting people she meets and the amusing experiences she has with them. She also describes fondly her favorite trees, mostly old ones with distinctive shapes and locations. She meditates on a bench near one of these arboreal friends.

I was her enthusiastic companion on the cool, drizzly fall day that Eileen walked the whole way around the lake for the first time after her move to the Hearthstone. She'd been working up to it for ten months and had gone what she judged to be halfway around many times. But she wanted moral support when she first braved the whole track.

Eileen gauged our progress by landmarks she'd passed many times. She was glad to have them described in more detail, and I was glad to meet the venerable trees she'd told me about. We stopped to rest on her meditation bench, which she estimated was at about the halfway point. Then we moved on into new territory. Even the increasing rain didn't dampen our spirits, as we rounded the last curve and started back toward the Hearthstone. I was a joyful witness to Eileen's accomplishment.

Walking at the lake is vital to Eileen's happiness and well-being at this stage of her life. She can get there without needing to drive a car. The glow she feels when she comes in from walking reinforces the decision she made to move to the retirement community, where she's assured of having a home for as long as she lives. Her time at the lake helps keeps her physically, mentally, and emotionally fit—and she can do it by herself!

Judith Starbuck

Chapter Five

Giving Up the Driver's Seat

Not drive?

How would I get to the post office, the grocery store, meetings, or my beloved beach place? Finally, though, I had to face the fact that I was a hazard on the road.

Even though I'd closed my ears to the occasional tactful remarks by family and friends, I'd realized for a while that I was becoming ever more high risk. I rationalized that I didn't drive at night or go on the freeway and drove only on familiar routes. I'd even passed a fairly recent driver's test. But I knew at some level that I should not be taking that car on the road.

Two or three minor episodes gave me pause, but not enough to quit. However, one dark, rainy afternoon, I failed to see a brightly dressed bicyclist well enough in advance and narrowly avoided hitting him. Fortunately, I was only a few blocks from home, because the incident really unnerved me. I gave myself a good talking to: "Don't drive under rainy conditions." It was more rationalizing.

Then, not more than a week later, I failed to see the young woman with a child in a stroller. Fortunately, she stopped as she entered the crosswalk right in front of me. Again, praise be, I avoided hitting them, but just barely. Again I was only a few blocks from home, but this time I put that big old car in the garage, patted her on her shiny, red rump, and said, "Honey, this is the last time I'll ever drive you!" And it was.

During all those months while I was driving when good sense told me I shouldn't be, it seems I had accepted the risk of involving myself in an accident. I'd failed to confront the possibility that I might injure or even kill someone. I still shudder to think how devastating this would have been and how it would have ruined the years I had left of my old age.

That left me with what seemed like an unanswerable question: "How do I manage my life when I don't drive?" The answers came from several sources.

I've Done It! What Now?

First, my younger son, then in his early fifties, came for the weekend to provide solace. That solace took the form of "Let's get practical, Mom. Let's make some lists. Let's look at family members to see what help they can provide. Let's make a list of friends who might be able to take you to the grocery store, to the doctor, to the post office. Let's look at public transportation. You've got two or three city buses practically at your door."

He said he thought there was federal legislation requiring that public transportation be provided for the elderly and disabled, and we should look into it. And he reminded me there are taxicabs. When I gulped at the idea of the expense, he replied, "But, Mom, what you're forgetting is you're not going to be putting out a lot of dollars a month to keep your car running, licensed, repaired, laundered, and parked."

"But how am I going to get to my beach cabin," I wailed. It was sixteen miles to the ferry, a twenty-five-minute ferry crossing and another twenty-five-minute drive on the other side. His suggestion for that: "How about paying a driver?" That seemed like madness to me. But again he brought me back with specifics. "Don't you know another older retired woman who needs to augment her income?"

Well, of course I did! Two women, longtime acquaintances, came to mind immediately. I called one the very next morning because getting to my beach place was my highest priority. She was not only interested; she wanted to know when we could start.

Specifics Help

By the time we finished these lists of possible helpers, I was feeling a bit more hopeful that life could go on without my very own wheels. I wasn't convinced, but I began to see there were options.

The next part of the answer came from a longtime friend and colleague, now retired, who I'd called right away to bemoan my plight. She sent me the most touching and supportive letter imaginable.

First, she thanked me for turning to her. Then she launched into the many things we could do together to which she could drive: grocery shopping once or twice a week, church meetings or retired faculty club activities at the university, day trips, concerts, and the symphony.

She would be happy to take me to doctors' appointments. And best of all, she could sometimes take me to the beach.

She loved that primitive place as much as I did, but, in my despair, I'd forgotten her deep affection for it.

Though I appreciated the many offers of "if there's anything I can do, let me know," the specifics my friend offered gave me something to latch onto. That's what I needed most at that moment.

Another friend penciled out for me a real eye-opener—what it was costing me to run that big old red car. Licensing in our state was very expensive; insurance was at a premium for an older driver, even with a good record; maintenance and repairs were costly; and there were all the unavoidables—tires, batteries, brakes, windshield wipers, headlights, mufflers, and gasoline. Parking and depreciation added many more dollars per month. And that didn't even include the toll it took on the environment.

How Did it Work Out? Help from Friends

So, fast-forward five years. Little by little, I've made the whole thing work. Not only have I found I can live without a car, but I'm relieved not to have all the responsibilities associated with one. I've also discovered there are many other options.

What about those specifics my son and friends suggested? First things first: getting to the beach. The retired woman I had called right away about driving me there quoted rates so low I felt I would be exploiting her, so we had a bit of a battle and came up with what seemed like a fair rate. And, by the way, she's been driving for me ever since. Her flexibility and willingness to take me at odd times make her invaluable. But an extra-special bonus is the deep friendship we've developed and the good times we've had, as she's provided me essential transportation.

Since I'd like to get to the beach more often than she or other regulars can take me, I've been getting into bartering. When friends ask to use the beach cabin for the weekend, I say, "Fine, and how about giving me a ride to the beach at another time in exchange?" So far this has been a win-win situation.

This leads me to my incredible friends. Help has been readily available, usually with just a telephone call, for doctors' appointments, errands, social events, meetings, and the double-duty trips to the grocery store, when a friend has to both drive and make selections for me. However, I've found it's easy to fall into the trap of asking too much from those who give so willingly, and I try to spread my requests out so I don't exploit anyone.

I've greatly appreciated the help of all kinds given by my many friends, but I've also had to learn not to expect it from everyone. Two or three of my longtime friends haven't offered to help, but they've shown their continuing friendship in many other ways that are more comfortable for them.

How Did It Work Out? All Those Other Suggestions

What about my experiences in using the various kinds of transportation suggested? Though I'd originally snorted at the idea, using the nearby city buses worked well until my vision and mobility deteriorated even further. Then I felt unsure about reading the number of the bus, getting off at the right place, and negotiating the steps. I gave up using public buses entirely when I began to use a walker. Though many buses are wheelchair-equipped, this added dimension made it too much for me to manage.

Sure enough, my son was right about the county providing transportation for the elderly and disabled. The county transportation agency provides Access buses, with door-to-door service for a minimal fee, from early morning to late at night. What a bargain, right? Well … it's a mixed blessing, but one I certainly would not want to do without, and I do use it frequently.

On the one hand, using Access requires a large amount of time, and since specific plans have to be in place at least twenty-four hours in advance, there's no spontaneous service. Their half-hour window for pickup often has to be as much as an hour before an appointment, allowing time for several other stops on the way. The return trip may take an hour or more while the bus drops off other people.

On the other hand, this is time during which I can do something productive and even enjoyable. I often walk, if the area where I'm being picked up is conducive to it, or I carry a bag with one of my little audio gadgets and put on my headphones to listen to music, poetry, a National Public Radio talk show, or news. And my son was also right that I can take a taxi several times a month for a lot less than the car would have cost me. It's a real comfort to be able to afford this occasional backup, especially when I can't make plans in advance. At other times, I just feel like indulging myself. We all need to indulge ourselves once in a while.

Why Did I Wait So Long?

As I look back, I wonder why my family and friends never talked to me openly about their concern over my driving. After the fact, my kids said I gave them the greatest gift when I quit. My friends also heaved a sigh of relief, and some even let me know I'd removed a burden from their shoulders. The depth of their concern was obvious from these reactions.

The closest I can remember to anyone confronting me was once when I was taking a friend to my beach cabin, and two or three times on the way and four or five times on the way back in the late afternoon, she offered rather insistently to drive. Did I let her? No! I still considered myself perfectly capable, it seems. I was closing my mind to the implications of her request.

I believe now that she felt insecure riding with me but didn't want to say anything that would offend me. She realized I was among the many aging people who find this a very touchy area.

Apparently my sons were in somewhat the same fix, talking together about their concern over my driving, but not ready to come right out and say I needed to think about quitting. I did frequently ask my younger son to critique my driving when he was with me. He wasn't ever frankly negative, but he wasn't strongly positive either. About the best I can remember him saying after a short trip together was, “I think you did okay, Mom.” I guess I let myself consider this sufficient approval for me to keep driving.

Pondering

How could the people who cared about me have broached this subject, those who after the fact expressed their relief? My son was probably reluctant to give an honest evaluation, sensing the defensiveness he might encounter, because I wasn’t ready to face what he had to tell me.

At that time it seemed to me that giving up driving would signal the end of my overall competence and independence. Now I see it didn’t mean that. My friends and family wanted to protect and help me, not restrict me without reason. Now I realize it wouldn’t have been an admission of weakness to let them advise me.

There’s no formula for dealing with this sticky issue; each of us has to do it in our own way. But I wish I’d been honest with myself in facing this challenge. I believe I should have stopped driving earlier than I did. I give thanks that I had the great good fortune to quit before I caused a tragedy I could not have lived with.

Chapter Six

Making the Move

"Oh, my, it's good to be home!"

I was amazed to hear myself say this when I walked into my apartment about five months after moving to the Hearthstone.

The decision to move to this retirement community from my much-loved condo wasn't easy. In fact, it took several years of indecisiveness. And once I'd moved, it took more time to adjust to a new way of life. But I did it, and I'm glad!

In many ways, this last move was harder than the one I had made after my husband died fifteen years earlier. Then I had left a lovely old brick Tudor, chock-full of the accumulations of fifty-plus years of marriage. But I didn't like living there alone. So when I heard through friends about a condo coming available in their building, I was ready to move. This fourth-floor apartment seemed to offer me everything I needed to start a new life: a view of water and mountains, friends in the building, secure indoor parking, a place down the hill to walk along the canal, even a Starbucks en route for my daily latte.

Resistance and Reality Testing

By contrast, I was afraid that if I moved to a retirement setting I'd have to give up my freewheeling way of life. In the condo, I had loved having my own space, keeping my own hours, welcoming friends into the privacy of my own home, getting up and going to bed when I wanted to, eating my meals at odd hours when I wanted to.

For a long time, I thought I could "age in place," continuing to live in the condo and getting additional help as I went along. But as time went by, I was less and less able to manage independently.

As my vision deteriorated, I needed help with reading mail, balancing the checkbook, reading the labels and sorting my medications, getting the right items at the grocery store, checking my clothes for spots, making sure I went out the door in matched shoes and earrings, and finding misplaced articles, which were in plain sight to those who could see.

The list went on—minor stresses fifty times a day. They would continue regardless of where I lived, but the accumulation of frustrations was taking its toll. I felt the need for more support.

Then I began to look realistically at my space. There wasn't enough room for the live-in help that would be needed eventually. That left me in limbo.

To a person, my friends said they didn't know why they had waited so long to move to a retirement home. Life was so much easier for them in their new setting. This held true whether they'd gone to a private retirement community or to subsidized or shared housing.

Then I had the opposite example in my friend Jody. She refused even to visit retirement facilities, although she fell frequently and had lost the strength to cook and dress herself. She did nothing to take charge of her own future while she was still able. She even fired the helpers who were brought in. After months of increasing resistance from her, her adult children felt compelled to move her against her will to the nursing home where she died a few months later.

Going through this agonizing experience with such a close friend and her family had a profound effect on me. I knew I had to make my own choices, had to take action while I was able.

Looking at Options

It soon became clear I had to do the legwork to search for alternatives. I was looking for greater security and better access to places where I could walk, where I wouldn't have to climb steep hills and cross busy streets. Also, I had to face the results of my vision loss; I was too high risk to myself and to others in my condo to cook any longer.

I looked at six or seven retirement facilities and put money down to hold a place in two of them. One was the kind that collects a monthly fee to provide services, which included twenty-five dinners a month. It had been started for university retirees and would be convenient and congenial. However, it provided independent and assisted living only.

The other, The Hearthstone, was the buy-in kind, requiring what for me was a sizable sum of money at the beginning, with a somewhat lower monthly fee. It had three levels of care—independent living, assisted living, and skilled nursing—and guaranteed lifelong tenure, even if a resident ran out of money.

An added advantage was the excellent location, which was important to me. My friends would have a relatively easy time visiting me there, and it was across the street from a beautiful lake in the heart of the city. I could walk on the path around the lake daily, and in front of the building there was a safe pedestrian-controlled crosswalk.

Money, Meals, and Cats

The Hearthstone seemed nearly ideal, but it had its disadvantages. I wondered whether it was prudent for a person in her late eighties to put so much money down. I might not live enough years to get my money's worth! If I had to move to assisted living, my expenses would mount rapidly. Each extra service—help with bathing, with dressing, with toileting—would add a separate fee. A la carte on a monthly basis seems to be standard for all such facilities.

Money was definitely an issue for me. When I was growing up, my mother and I were often nearly destitute. That, and living through the Great Depression, have given me a deep-seated fear of running out of money. I had to give myself a little lecture. I told myself that unless I lived to be 101, I probably wouldn't run out.

I did have enough money for the buy-in. My children were adamant that what I could leave to them was not to be the main consideration. According to them, making my decision to move while I could still enjoy my new living arrangement was worth a substantial investment—an investment in my quality of life and their peace of mind.

On a more mundane note, the thought of going down to the dining room three times a day seemed like a negative. I knew I didn't want to socialize at breakfast. And there would be times I'd want to eat dinner with only Jim Lehrer on The NewsHour for company. Being sociable at every meal seemed daunting. Also, I was afraid I'd embarrass myself when my low vision caused me to knock over a cup of coffee or make a mess around my plate.

Among all the considerations in choosing where to live, one of the most important was Tanya, my cat. None of the retirement facilities I visited would allow even lovely kitties like her. Though at eighteen she did have a few problems, she was sweet and loving good company. I'd been close to her for so long I couldn't imagine putting her down because I had to live somewhere else. Nor could I imagine trying to give her away. Those who had offered to take her had cats themselves, and Tanya was never going to be a beta cat! I know non-cat people can't imagine how I could let this influence me, but it was a very real part of my dilemma.

Right Place, Right Time

As it turned out, an important condition that had held up a move was that I hadn't been offered the right apartment. That's what finally tipped the scales.

First, I got a wake-up call. A Pyrex baking dish I'd accidentally set on a hot burner blew up, sending glass all over the kitchen and beyond. Almost simultaneously, the Hearthstone sent a letter and pictures announcing two openings. One sounded almost perfect, and I went immediately to see it. I walked onto its deck. There was a fabulous view over the lake and trees. I fell in love. But for some reason I still agonized. I hung on for a bit longer to the myth that my condo was still offering me the quality of life it had given me for ten years.

Then I faced the facts. It was not. Several of my closest friends had moved out of my building. I could no longer walk safely outside because of uneven pavement, steep hills, and busy streets. It wasn't safe to cook, so the entertaining

I'd previously enjoyed was out. I needed to downsize and get rid of a lot of stuff so I could manage better.

Finally I let go of the myth. I would move! Right away I started making arrangements with the Hearthstone marketing staff. A few weeks later I signed on the dotted line, committing myself to this place where I expect to live the rest of my life.

Downsizing, selling the condo, getting ready, and moving seemed insurmountable. But everything fell into place with the help of a senior-services professional from my church. She did everything. She shepherded me through packing, selling or donating what I didn't want to keep, and setting up in my new place. Services like hers are increasingly available, and I highly recommend them. Expensive? Yes, but worth it in the long run.

My children were so grateful I didn't have to use their strong backs and precious time for this move. They gave me great support in other ways, as did many of my friends. I recommend all of them highly, but they're not for hire. Theirs was a gift of caring.

Time Has Told

For the first few weeks after I moved, I wondered if I'd be able to adapt. Could I learn to live differently, accept the situation, and not dwell on the things that bothered me? As I went along, I realized time was taking care of many of my misgivings. As the unfamiliar became familiar, these misgivings disappeared, one by one.

One of the biggest adjustments was having to meet "all those people!" This seemed overwhelming at first. Now I see it as a real plus. I enjoy the general atmosphere of goodwill, pleasant greetings, and lively people at dinner. I'm amazed how energetic some of those in their upper nineties and early one hundreds are. I get almost universal comments that people here seem happy.

People have sorted themselves out. Lillian, a retired child psychiatrist, and I, with my years of research in child development, immediately found we had much in common. Winifred invited me to her place to listen to music. Bill always has a quip about our group lifestyle. I discovered it was easy to make friends.

One person I met in a more comical way. We locked horns, or more specifically walker handles, getting on the elevator. We got a round of applause when we finally got untangled and let the other riders get to where they were going.

The aroma of corn popping on Monday afternoons draws many of us to the activities room, where we enjoy each other's company while nibbling on popcorn from red-and-white striped bags. Several residents have offered to read to me. Sharing mutually interesting books and articles turns out to be a rewarding way to spend an afternoon or evening with my in-house neighbors.

There are lots of Hearthstone activities I can sample when I'm not so involved elsewhere. I'm already participating in a group for residents interested in writing stories about their lives. The teacher gives encouraging feedback, and I'm finding this activity is an unexpected way of getting to know others with similar interests. As a bonus, the teacher wants to work with me to write down some of my stories, since I can't do it myself.

Meals no longer present the difficulties I once envisioned. Taking some of my meals in the dining room is a pleasure. A well-stocked salad bar at both lunch and dinner gives me a choice of soups, salads, fruits, and desserts to take to my room for when I feel like being on my own. The staff is cooperative, and I try to be careful not to ask for too many special favors.

My apartment is feeling more and more like home. I have my balcony with plants and flowers on it. I still have my old red desk and big old bookcases to give me a sense of continuity. I can go to bed when I want. And I can still have friends and my church group over in the privacy of my own place.

Not a day goes by during which I don't feel grateful that I can walk around the lake, watch the seasons change, be part of the bustle and energy, and keep fit. Proximity to the lake, more than anything, drew me to this place. It has cinched my belief that I made the right decision to move here.

A Happy Ending

The Tanya story also has a happy ending. By the time I made the decision to move, she had gone downhill and was looking her age, sleeping most of the time, and not eating well. She had some undesirable habits that made me reluctant to give her to someone else. With considerable anguish, I decided the best thing for both of us would be to have her put to sleep.

My senior-services helper told me about a veterinarian who would come to the apartment to administer the lethal dose. He was tender and gentle with Tanya, and with me, throughout the procedure. I was able to stroke her gently until she drew her last breath. I had the satisfaction of knowing I'd given her a good life and had seen her quiet and contented to the end. For cat or human, how much better to end life before sickness and trauma turn it into a painful nightmare. I felt I had done the right thing and have had no regrets.

Adapting to being here in my new apartment and to being without Tanya was easier because there was nothing to remind me of her in my new digs. There was no Tanya in the corner, no Tanya curled up in her favorite chair, no Tanya to trip over.

Pondering

When I surprised myself by saying, "Oh, my, it's good to be home," I realized that after five months I did feel at home and was glad to be here. I'd found the right setting to live the last years of my life. I'm less harried and more secure. I can now agree with all the friends who said, "I don't know why I didn't move sooner." This simpler life, with fewer worries and frustrations, gives me a glimpse of what it's like to live in the now. Every day I'm filled with gratitude for the contentment this way of life provides.

I don't have to worry about what's to become of me. I will not subject myself or my family to the wrenching experience of Jody and her family. Best of all, I made my own decision and orchestrated the move, with lots of help, of course. I can no longer be independent, but even at ninety, I'm happy that, for a while longer, at least, I can trust myself to make sound decisions.

Chapter Seven

Living Independently: Myth or Reality

Is independence a myth?

Is there any way I could function entirely on my own, at my age, and with my limitations? Of course not! But does that mean I relinquish all control over my life? Should I now follow all the well-meaning advice of everyone who wishes to keep me safe and secure? Should I stay inside on rainy days and keep as much money in the bank as possible, even when a family member is in trouble? I think not!

What is the reality? I'm certainly far from helpless. I suppose it's a question of how we define independence.

For me independence has three dimensions. The first, and probably the most important, is doing as much for myself as I can. The second, what I think of as autonomy, is trusting myself and being trusted to make decisions about how I want to live my old age. And last, but not least, is acknowledging that to preserve as much independence as possible, I must accept the help I clearly do need.

In other words, it's important to hang onto the things we can still do and manage our everyday lives so they reflect who we are. It's equally important to make our own decisions, before it's too late and someone else has to make the decisions for us. Then recognizing and accepting help when we need it frees us to put our remaining resources to good use.

Getting Help

There are so many things I can do perfectly well for myself, and yet I need help in so many ways. How do I balance accepting the help I truly need and diverting help where I feel I can manage for myself? And if I turn away help now, how do I keep lines open for the help I may need six months or two years from now? After all, my blindness and deafness aren't going to go away, nor is my old age.

The balance is increasingly weighted on the help-I-truly-need end. One or the other of my children helps me with bills and finances. When I'm out for lunch with a friend, I try to include a few errands—stopping at the post office, finding a birthday card, or getting cash at the bank. I enlist friends who visit to take a few minutes to help sort my mail into "recycling," "to pay," "to do," "to file," or "to think upon."

Everybody who comes gets to help put my calendar in order. This is not your everyday little pocket reminder. It's a bunch of 8½ x 11-inch loose pages with big writing, arranged in chronological order—or at least they're supposed to be. They're in perpetual need of reordering, with new pages to add and old ones to clear out. And I admit I do occasionally drop the whole thing on the floor …

Then there are the one-minute chores, like reading two or three labels, changing my hearing aid batteries, deciphering an illegible note I've left myself, looking up a phone number, or identifying mysterious objects.

Friends and family have marked the On buttons with Velcro on my tape and CD players and TV remotes, because none seem to work the same way. I still can't remember which works which way and have to rehearse repeatedly with whoever is on the spot.

Helping Myself

The list of times I need help could go on and on, and, even so, I still have innumerable situations where I must devise solutions myself to cope with or to reduce frustrations. When I spill a three-pound bag of frozen blueberries, getting them up off the floor is a major chore. And rarely is there a friend around at 7:00 AM when I'm having breakfast. I coach myself to immediately put the twisty back on the bag, but the one time I forget …

On the "do-it-myself" end of the scale, I still prepare my breakfasts, keep my schedule in a semblance of order, arrange for rides, and generally get to places on time. I still do my own laundry, but it's a challenge. Not only do I have to remember all the dials on the washer and dryer, but I also have to follow the protocol. Each floor has a tidy laundry facility, and residents on the floor set up the guidelines that make it work for everybody.

The first rule is: You never take out someone else's laundry because you think it's dry. I did that early in my time at the Hearthstone, and almost as soon as I got back to my apartment the phone was ringing. A resident I hadn't yet met was sputtering and fuming, informing me that "you just don't take anyone else's laundry out!" My explanation that it had seemed dry and I'd carefully stacked it on top was to no avail. I finally apologized, and that was the end of it. But I learned my lesson on that score.

I have, however, persuaded people to give me a dispensation regarding the laundry card file. Each resident's apartment number is on one card for the washer and another for the dryer. The card is pulled and left in an envelope on the machine to show which resident is using it. The cards are filed in a box in apartment-number order. Since I can't see to find my cards, I leave mine all the way at the back. A note asking the tidy souls who had been refiling them to leave my cards at the back is so far working.

I handle many of my affairs pretty well, but more and more, I'm making decisions that others help me to carry out. And sometimes I just need to let go. I've had to accept that there are things I can no longer do. Of course, the main one was driving. Other things I've had to give up are cooking, walking alone in unfamiliar places, and the ballet, symphony, and theater that require better vision and hearing than I have.

Autonomy

Old age hasn't changed my commitment to the things that really matter to me. If anything, it has deepened my dedication to family, church, friends, and work—all things that have sustained me for so many years. Now that I'm old, do I stop making decisions in these areas, because others may know better?

No! But do I consult my children and close friends about major life decisions? Of course! And I listen closely to their advice. I even double-check with them sometimes, asking, "This isn't a crazy decision, is it?"

It's becoming more and more important to make sure my choices are based on reality rather than some mythical ideal left over from what I used to be able to do. A good example is my beach place. I have to ask myself, "Is it realistic or reckless to stay there alone?" If I take the stand that I can still manage, what precautions do I need to take so I don't jeopardize the self-sufficiency I still have? I cannot afford to be foolhardy. I have to prove I can be trusted.

I've already had to accept that I can no longer take long, solitary walks on my isolated beach if I want to keep going there at all. What else? I tell my family and friends, who are rightfully concerned, about the safeguards I've put in place. I wear a lifeline that calls the next-door neighbors first, and if they're not home, successively calls three others within ten minutes' drive of my beach house. I carry a cell phone at all times, programmed to call 911 with a flip of the lid. I use my walker whenever I'm outside. I use only the microwave and the oven, and don't use the burners on the stove when there's no one else there.

Help Is Not Always Helpful

Even after I've recovered from the blow to my self-image that accepting help represents, there are other challenges. I've come to understand that appropriate help isn't intuitive for many people who truly want what's best for me. Let me vent a bit with a few examples of what I've found frustrating, even objectionable.

Someone takes me by the elbow of the arm I'm using for my cane, obviously not understanding that this throws me off balance and causes me to walk with less assurance. A well-meaning friend takes hold of my walker and imposes her pace on me, not noticing that this renders my walker useless and means I'm sometimes unable to keep up.

Once I nearly blew my stack in a restaurant when a frequent companion, without a word to me, gathered up my packages and purse and marched off to the cash register. There I was, madly searching for my possessions I didn't know were no longer there. My friend didn't realize how hard I'd worked to make sure I knew how many pieces I had to take care of. I routinely rehearse what I'm carrying with me when I leave home and add to my mental list as I acquire a thing or two or three.

One more example shows even more graphically how someone holding to her own notion of what is helpful can cause real anguish. At a potluck with a large group of women, a friend took me through the buffet line and helped me identify various foods. This assistance was much appreciated—if only she had stopped there …

When we got to the table, she advised me that the chicken had a bone in it and offered to cut mine up. I told her thanks, but I could manage. When she insisted, I refused a little more firmly. Fixed on her version of what was helpful, she stood up, leaned across the table, long necklace dangling in my plate, and cut up the chicken into child-sized bites.

I realize now that she was not able to put herself in my place and understand that her action was actually demeaning. But at the time I wanted to explode like a red-faced, frustrated toddler and push the helpful hand away, screaming, "Me do it, me do it!"

Learned Helplessness

It might seem like a small matter to just let people do things for me. Sure, it's quicker, neater, and less trouble for the person who can see to do it. But since I don't always have someone at my elbow when a need arises, I consider it essential to maintain skills to keep from falling into "learned helplessness." Sometimes I catch myself thinking, "I'll leave this until one of my friends comes." But I feel so much better about myself if I go ahead and do it, even if it takes lots longer. And it means I can keep doing it. I won't lose it, because I'll use it.

I've heard that if I keep trying to do something, like plug in a coffeepot, this maintains my eye-hand coordination, and my brain helps out. And not only that, I have to admit I get a kick out of inventing new ways to remember where I hung my favorite jacket in my closet, to find my walnuts after I put them away, or to heat up my coffee in the microwave.

Is it worth it to fight so hard to maintain as much independence as possible? Yes! I still picture myself as a capable, self-sufficient, energetic person, even though I know I'm not the going concern I once was. I seem to have the same drive as that two- or three-year-old struggling desperately to achieve independence. Now I'm working just as desperately to maintain as much independence as possible—to do as much for myself as I possibly can for as long as I possibly can.

Yes, it is worth it—for my morale, my incentive, my enjoyment of life, my self-image. I have to admit, I love the plaudits I get for being so independent. But this independence wouldn't exist without all the help I get from family and friends.

What Message Do I Give?

What does this mean for how I interact with others?

I have a recent example that really set me thinking about this in very specific ways. I went with a new friend to a sculpture park that had just opened on the waterfront. She and I hadn't spent time together before, and I hadn't given her any hints about what kind of help I needed to negotiate this unfamiliar terrain, which included sunken terraces invisible to me. We'd been walking for only a few minutes when I stepped off a low wall I couldn't see was there and went flying head over heels, walker and all, to what seemed like almost-certain catastrophe.

Fortunately the ground was soft from the new construction. I was only shaken up and bruised, though it took several minutes to get my breath back and to realize that I was okay. I was amazed, as were several concerned onlookers and my friend, to discover that I hadn't been seriously injured.

Later, I thought about how I could have averted this fall and what it meant for future forays into unfamiliar settings.

I realized I'd given my friend very mixed messages about how she could be helpful. I'd shaken off her attempts to take my arm, probably indicating to her I could manage on my own. She didn't know how little I could see and assumed I didn't need a warning that I was about to step into space. Of course, everybody involved felt terrible, and I decided I had to learn from this.

It's a Plan

Here's my plan. Whenever I'm going with a friend into an unfamiliar place, I need to ask to take her arm. I can even say this is only until I learn my way. I need to let others know what is helpful to me, not just push away what I don't find helpful. It's even gone through my mind to have a list. I probably wouldn't ever give it to anyone, but it would help me think about what I need and how to convey this to others in a positive way. It might read like this.

Please:

Wait for me to take your arm instead of taking my cane arm. This will keep me from being thrown off balance.

Walk beside my walker as I use it, and walk at my pace (though you can remind me to stand up straight if you want).

Do offer to help, but wait for me to ask for what I need. If you have something in mind you think might be helpful, ask if I'd like that help.

Pay attention to what I can do for myself, and practice patience while I do it.

Try to imagine how you would feel if you were in my position.

By all means, if I'm about to walk over a cliff or in front of a car, shout, grab me, and do anything necessary to avert disaster.

Pondering

This drive I have to maintain my independence is not based on vanity or a need to make a better show. It springs from a deeply felt commitment to preserving my ability to do as much for myself as long as I can. At the same time, I need to continue to honestly assess where I am in this aging process. The day may come when I'll no longer be able to live in the independent living section of the Hearthstone. The point is to delay asking for help with bathing, dressing, and getting to the dining room as long as possible and then to accept more help if it becomes necessary.

In the meantime, I want to give friends and family the whole picture:

- I appreciate what they do for me immensely.
- I promise I will ask for help when I see that I need it.
- I will be as realistic as possible so they can trust my decisions.
- I will give as many specifics as I can for how they can help me preserve maximum independence, as I've defined it.

Something I must never lose track of is the fact that I have as much responsibility to understand the people who help me as they have to understand me. It's a two-way street. I realize I cannot expect to have it my way all the time. I need to respond to the goodwill of others with the flexibility I expect of them. Each relationship is different.

For some people, I have to let them help me their way, because it's so important to their self-image. If I want to keep these people in my life, I have to accept help the way it's offered. It's important to them to anticipate another's needs, and the idea of waiting for me to ask seems to make them feel negligent.

For some people, it's a real gift to be given an opportunity to help in a meaningful way. I must remember that by trying to be so fiercely independent, I may be denying the pleasure many others experience in giving.

As I've found in life in general, sometimes a sense of humor will be the way through any problems that arise.

I must go on giving proof I can be trusted, so I can go on making my own decisions. Does this sound like I'm headstrong and stubborn? Well, maybe I am. But my family and friends seem to appreciate my making my own decisions and not putting that responsibility on them. I don't think they really want to run my life and make my decisions for me. As my son says, "It's much more fun to advise the queen than to run the country."

I will count on their advice and help to make this independence so essential to me a reality based on good judgment and mutual respect rather than a myth based on wishful thinking and outgrown beliefs.

Chapter Eight

Staying Fit Is More Than Sit-Ups

"Use it or lose it!"

That's one of those age-old clichés I firmly believe.

I'm convinced keeping fit is crucial to a good old age. But it means more than the daily walk or going to the gym. It means engaging the mind and spirit as well. My own experience is confirmed by current research that shows we need body, mind, and spirit working together to keep us involved and lively.

Let me take these one at a time.

— *Physical Fitness* —

Physical fitness is more than sit-ups. It's never too late to discover which activity suits each of us and get started. My first love is walking. For some, it's working out in a gym or running. For others, it's gardening (even pot gardening on the deck), vacuuming, and other household chores. Others may find swimming—laps or water exercises—more to their liking. And daily chair exercises are good for those with limited strength and mobility.

It seems the older we get the harder it gets to push ourselves. I've noticed inertia does set in. I sometimes have to give myself a real pep talk to get out the door, or even to get up out of my chair to head toward it. But once I'm out there, even for a little while, all the benefits kick in. Research is showing that as little as thirty minutes of some kind of physical activity daily can improve our strength and balance, no matter how old we are.

Keeping active in one way or another has been important to me at every stage of my life. It's one of the underlying factors of my good old age. It seems to me that a major reason I've had good health most of my life is because I've walked and walked and walked.

It started out as necessity. Like so many families in the 1920s and 1930s, we didn't have a car. My children still remember my saying, "Let's galvanize; let's get out of here," for a walk or an errand. The habit has stuck with me throughout my life. I know that not everybody's a walker, but, lucky me—I really enjoy it!

In Training

My new living situation at the Hearthstone means that Green Lake is just a few steps away. Eighty years ago I learned to swim there as a skinny, shivering eight-year-old. Two of my children learned to swim at the same beach. For several years I walked the nearly three miles around it regularly. I figured I wouldn't be doing that anymore. But then I said to myself, "What kind of attitude is that? Why don't you put yourself in training?"

"What a ridiculous idea," I said back to myself. "I can't do that at my age." Nevertheless, I made the decision to give it a try, using my walker, of course.

It started out as a step-counting process. Next time I went to the lake, I counted the steps in the distance I'd been going already. It was four hundred steps, probably a couple of short city blocks, but it was a start.

It was mid-spring. My self-initiated training program was a simple one. I would walk at least one hundred steps farther each week. The one hundred steps seemed to motivate rather than tire me, and, before I knew it, I was walking three hundred extra steps each week.

How many steps would it take to go a mile? My son discovered it was a mile between two landmarks I could readily recognize. I counted several times and found it took about two thousand of my steps to go that mile. That meant that halfway around the lake was about three thousand steps.

By early fall I was getting close to that three thousand steps, then turning around and returning to where I had started. I knew it was time to just keep walking all the way around.

After one of our work sessions on the book, Judith came with me to make the ceremonial circumnavigation, complete with fruit juice, crackers, and cheese in the basket of my walker—just in case I ran out of steam. And I made it—all the way around, with only one rest stop! What a great feeling it was.

Now, more than a year later, I go clear around the lake about once a week, so I know I can still do it. Other days

I usually walk a mile or mile and a half. My son, who sees me every few weeks, says he's noticed such a difference in my carriage and walking.

Rounding Out the Exercise Picture

In addition to walking, I do leg exercises which were recommended to me when I had a knee replacement. Following this discipline has surely paid off. I've had no postoperative problems. Also, I use odd moments to keep using my muscles—a dozen toe raises while I'm waiting alone for the elevator in my building, tensing my abdominal muscles or doing Kegels anywhere.

After a few near falls, it's become clear I need to improve my balance. And upper body strength is increasingly important. How am I going to get myself up off the floor if I fall? Fortunately there's a trainer downstairs available to all residents. She designed a program for me to work on balance and strength and taught me what to do. Now it's up to me.

This brings me to the many resources which are available to all of us. We can go to senior centers for activities ranging from yoga and aerobics to chair exercises. Many HMOs, including mine, offer a variety of fitness programs. There are swimming pools at community centers and parks; I used one for years when I was swimming regularly. There are TV programs and videotapes for those who can see. One of the advantages of having moved to my retirement center is the availability of a well-equipped exercise room and the exercise coaching I mentioned.

When we sit for long periods, we can lose our mobility. In fact, I've learned that too much sitting robs me of my strength and often contributes to dependency. Whenever I can, I pass up offers of help and go to get my drink of water, my tissue, or my sweater myself. I find that the more I move, the more energy I seem to have. It's giving in to that lurking inertia that robs me of it!

— *Mental Fitness* —

Just as physical fitness is more than sit-ups, mental fitness is more than crossword puzzles. Research shows that including a variety of mental gymnastics keeps different parts of the brain active. There's no such thing as saving space in our memories for "the important things." Memory is not governed by capacity but by how much we ask of it and how well we keep exercising it.

Most of us experience some memory loss as we age, but we can slow the process by engaging in mental activities. Here are some of mine.

It's helpful for me to mull over a National Public Radio program, a book on tape, or a lecture or sermon, to try to find ways to apply it to my life. When I want to add another dimension beyond mulling things over myself, I can always talk with interesting people among my family and friends. They're in Crone conversation groups and my church covenant group. A friend comes weekly to read and talk about poetry or books. Often we veer off into discussions about life. Sometimes lively discussions happen at the dinner table in the downstairs dining room. Open seating provides different combinations of my neighbors each night.

To help myself pay attention and concentrate, I mentally underline points I want to remember, and then I rehearse. When I put my hearing aid down other than in its usual place, I go over and over its new location. I review each morning what's on my week's calendar to fix it in my mind. I enjoy committing my grocery list to memory, using groupings of fruits, vegetables, and meats. When I'm introduced to someone new, I use the name two or three times in conversation and then again when I say good-bye.

I charge myself with carrying away at least one thought when I leave a lecture or sermon, and then I play it over later.

I've always enjoyed games of all sorts, like the ones I used to play with my kids on long car journeys. It sounds silly, but I still keep my mind busy with word and number games, such as saying the alphabet backward, reciting three girls' names starting with each letter of the alphabet, doing simple math problems, or figuring the tip in my head.

I try to solve simple problems. For example, when I told our medical driver I had a daughter who was sixty-six, he said he'd have to live to be ninety-nine to see his daughter that old. He said his daughter was thirteen in 2006. I set for myself the problem of figuring out how old he was at that time. (Did you get it? It's forty-six.)

Hanging in There

I almost gave up memorizing poetry, even though it had become such a mainstay of my life. It seemed like too great a challenge when I had to switch from large print to audio tapes and CDs. The constant mechanical intrusion of rewinding, fast-forwarding, and playing was so distracting. But there was no other way, so I kept at it. Now auditory learning has become almost as comfortable as the way I learned before. I'm so glad I hung in there and didn't give up.

Because of this experience, I coach myself to stick with a challenge. Any time I can resolve a problem on my own, I feel better about myself. And I get results, even if it's just getting the plug into the outlet so I can listen to NPR on the radio.

I'm particularly lucky to have this book to work on. I thought my writing days were over when I couldn't write down my thoughts and see to edit them as I used to. I couldn't imagine dictating and sending the words into what seemed like a void. Then Judith became part of the process, and I found dictating to a real, live person could be exciting and fun. It's stimulating to look together for the right words and ways to say clearly what I have in mind. Talk about mental exercise!

There are things I can't do. This I do have to accept. I need to give up before I get too frustrated. There will be no talking computers for me. I couldn't master them after several weeks of heroic effort.

— *Spiritual Fitness* —

If physical fitness is more than sit-ups, and mental fitness is more than crossword puzzles, is spiritual fitness more than going to church? For me it is.

What do I mean by spiritual? In my mind, it has to do with the essence of each of us, with what makes us who we are, determines our relationships to the world around us, makes us unique. It is reflected in our reactions, our interactions with family and friends, our compassion, our gratitude, and our joy in living. And it is reflected in our awareness.

Spiritual fitness takes a different kind of awareness than mental fitness does. For me, spiritual fitness is taking note of simple, everyday events and the people I meet, live with, and interact with. It's paying attention to things that bring joy: the finch that perched on my railing and gave me a fragment of song before it flicked its tail and flew away; the feel of the bark—shaggy, mossy, smooth—on the trees I love to touch on my walk; and the people I meet on the path around the lake—all colors, shapes, and ages.

Spiritual fitness means having things in my life which nourish me. Number one is getting to my beach place as often as I can. There I immerse myself in the nature I love so much. Another priority is spending time with friends, with all the variety they have to offer. Still another is listening to CDs and tapes that inspire me or make me laugh or cry. Just as important is spending time alone, dipping into meditation, which I've never felt I had time to do before. I affirm the person I want to be, reflect on what's going on, and, even as old as I am, look toward the future.

Encounters

By a spiritual exercise as simple as opening up to others, I often have extraordinary experiences. One time a young woman, April, who had just graduated from nursing school, came up to me while I was having a latte at Starbucks. She asked if she could sit with me. I told her I was deep in thought, and suggested "maybe another time." She moved off to a table nearby. Almost immediately I asked myself, "Why did I do that? There may not be another time." So I got up and told her, "I don't know why I said that. Would you still join me?" With a smile, she picked up her latte and came to sit with me. We ended up having a lively and enjoyable conversation that lasted for an hour and a half, and we parted as friends.

I never saw her again. She was leaving the next day for her home in New Jersey, where she had a job waiting. Though we haven't kept in touch as we'd promised, this is one example of a spiritual connection that will live in my heart forever, and probably also in hers. I feel joy whenever I think of that opportunity I almost missed. I followed an impulse, changed my mind, and then got such a payoff.

These human connections are major contributors to my spiritual fitness. It's so important to be open to them, whether they are destined to enrich for a few moments, as with April, or ripen over a long time, as with Elaine, my friend for more than fifty years. Most of us can testify that having friends keeps our spirits up.

Being My Own Friend

Last, but certainly not least, I'm realizing how important it is to believe in myself, feel good about myself, and trust myself. The concept of self-worth eluded me during the first part of my life. One of the hardest things for me to let go of was putting myself down. But, oh, what a difference when I consider what I like about myself instead of what I don't! It's kind of a spiritual lift when I can say to myself, "You're okay, old girl!" Admittedly, I have to keep working on this, because those old mind-sets keep whispering otherwise.

I realize also that my accomplishments are not what make me worthwhile. I no longer berate myself for not getting enough done. For example, at night, now, instead of lamenting over what I didn't get done that day, I've taken to congratulating myself for what I've accomplished, even if it's only a little.

Pondering

Keeping body, mind, and spirit in sync creates the foundation of an all-around healthy old age. I've discussed each separately, but they're intertwined. The activities we engage in with friends often involve all three. I remember ferocious battles over the Scrabble board. Scrabble with my dear friend of forty-five years not only provided mental and spiritual exercise, but even physical exercise as we jumped up frequently to consult the heavyweight dictionary on its stand across the room.

True, as we age we can't always exercise all three aspects equally, but it's important to keep doing what we can, and even to push ourselves a little in each. I tell myself, if I can only take a walk in the hallway, start a conversation in the elevator, and listen to a favorite story, I'll do those things today—and, I hope, again tomorrow and the next day.

All three aspects of overall fitness require appre-ciation of self and others. They all involve taking responsibility for oneself and being engaged with others. It's never too late to try something new, to flex those muscles and brain cells to keep fit in body, mind, and spirit in our old age.

Section Three

How can slowing down in old age be such a plus?

Setting the Scene: The Hearthstone

It's a welcoming place. The residents are out and about in the halls or in the elevators. They're on their way to the dining room, the exercise room, a lecture in the chapel, or outside for a walk or shopping. Some may not be moving very fast and may be using walkers and canes, but they're moving.

When I visit Eileen at the Hearthstone, the first thing I see when I get out of the elevator is a collage of pictures lovingly assembled by Eileen's neighbor across the hall to celebrate the appropriate season. It's obvious the people who live here care about the place they call home.

Eileen's apartment clearly shows her touch: one wall is

lined with books, and her collection of interesting bowls, baskets, and folk art is placed tastefully here and there. There are flowers on the table if any are to be had. A huge dictionary always has a place of honor on its stand. Though she often apologizes for what a mess her place is, it always looks relatively neat to me. "A place for everything and everything in its place" has become a necessity with her low vision.

I often join her for lunch in the Hearthstone's dining room. On the way to our favorite table by the window, we check out the salad bar with its appetizing and ample offerings. Eileen often brings a bag to carry home her cookies (and mine, too, if I don't want them) and containers of soup and salad for her evening meal at home while watching The NewsHour with Jim Lehrer.

Eileen feels that she has a life in perfect balance at the Hearthstone. She can savor a slower pace and time alone. She can join any of the variety of activities offered when she chooses. There are interesting people at hand to socialize with almost any time, as well as family and old friends who visit. Here, where she knows she'll never have to move again, she can take stock of her long life, in the solitude her pleasant home offers or with others who have much in common with her.

Judith Starbuck

Chapter Nine

Savoring Life in the Slow Lane

Less is more.

When this saying was popular forty years ago, I really didn't get it. I was just hitting my stride, gaining recognition in my profession, adding one exciting new adventure after another. Those words didn't speak to me. Now I really understand them. Now I'm finding joy in living them.

Back then, when my "to do" list defined my life, things like enjoying nature and getting better acquainted with myself seldom made it to the top. Now that I'm doing a lot less, these very things seem to me the most fulfilling. What could be a higher priority than taking time to watch the acrobatics of the house swallows as they dart and dive?

I'm so glad I don't have to berate myself for just sitting and watching, for losing myself in thought, for enjoying my own company. I can't charge around, managing six things at once, even if I want to. But I don't want to.

Instead, I revel in sitting on my deck in the morning sun. This bird—LBJ (little brown job)—keeps singing the same song, much to my delight and his. I find myself smiling. Just to be part of the sunshine and birdsong is all I need at that moment. I feel fulfilled.

Being fully in these moments now seems as important as the "doing" that ruled me in earlier days. When I finally rouse myself, I feel I've accomplished something miraculous. I've found a part of myself that's apparently been there all along, but I've never met before. I welcome the time to let my scattered parts ease together like some living jigsaw puzzle.

My enjoyment of less includes two parts: fewer activities and less stuff.

— *Activities* —

I'm not just sitting around, piecing myself together. Though I don't want to schedule too much, there are still activities I want to keep in my life. I'm learning to make adjustments so I can.

Interactions at the Lake

As I mentioned in an earlier chapter, I've been walking around the lake since the day I moved into the Hearthstone. With my walker I move slowly, but there are positive sides to that.

Because I'm not rushing, I find I'm tuning in to what's happening around me in a way I previously didn't. I smile at passersby as they smile at me; I admire the babies in their strollers with their pretty young moms, ponytails flying, or dads with babes on their backs; I marvel at the parade of dogs, from chihuahuas to Great Danes. Of course, I don't actually "see" most of this. But after I take a peripheral glimpse, my mind's eye fills in the rest.

My walker has a seat, so if I want to gaze longer at something, I can linger and sit down if I need to. This allows me to savor the chance encounters that turn out to mean so much to me.

I wouldn't have wanted to miss the time I met an old gent walking with his two miniature terriers. As I stopped my walker to get out of their way, he said, "I want to introduce you to my 'watch dogs.'" I must have registered my incredulity, giving him the opening to say, "They're Rolex and Timex." Or the time a little girl, maybe four, walking with her mother, was fascinated with my walker. I asked, "Would you like your Mommy to give you a ride on it?" She said yes. After they came back and we'd chatted for a little while, she fished in her pocket for a tiny, shiny piece of wood. She said she wanted me to have it and pressed it into my hand. I treasure it to this day.

A Few Special Groups

Finding a way to stay involved with a few groups that really matter to me is also a high priority. I've invited my church covenant group to hold its meetings in my small apartment. It turns out the cozy space gives all nine of us a sense of belonging and feeling involved.

I don't have to miss out on the news of what goes on where I live. Dorothy reads the house newsletter to several of us at the first of every month. As well, as I mentioned earlier, I participate in the writing group at the Hearthstone.

Then there's Crone. Friends drive me to meetings and activities and offer help when I need it. Though I've had to give up board and newsletter staff positions, I find other ways to stay involved. I participate in programs and help plan special events. At a recent program on humor, I decided to do an over-the-top dramatic reading of a Dorothy Parker poem, "One Perfect Rose." I ended by throwing a red rose over my shoulder with a constipated look on my face. To my delight, it brought the house down.

The Beach, of Course

Spending time at my beach cabin is a special challenge. People ask, "What do you do up there all alone?"

I say, "I be." I've had to cut back my activities there to the bone. I no longer allow myself to walk alone on the beach. I know I'm high risk for a fall on the shifting sand and random rocks, and there would be no one to pick me up. A broken hip would be devastating.

But I've discovered something marvelous. Sitting on my weathered old bench just above the high-tide mark, I get a lot of vicarious pleasure out of experiencing all that goes on: the ebbing tides, the play of light on the cliffs, a heron fishing, a gaggle of shorebirds doing their line dance, the otter pups cavorting on the big rock. When someone says, "There's a heron," I have an instant pop-up memory. During the many years I walked miles along the beach or waded in the shallows, I was engaged actively. Now the images remain, and I feel I'm still involved, but in a different way.

I also have my beloved garden at the beach place. I now hire a gardener to do what I used to enjoy doing for hours myself. I find gardening has become less rewarding as I can't see to pick flowers for bouquets, and I pull up "weeds" that turn out to be perennial poppies coming up from seed.

Actually, it's kind of a relief to let the vegetable garden and all but a small cultivated area go "back to nature." The indigenous snowberry and red-flowering currant that are creeping in will survive, because they belong.

These native plants are a part of nature I'm getting to know again. They take me back to my childhood, when I walked in wooded areas more common in big cities then, looking for the thimbleberry and currant that were harbingers of spring. Part of why I love my beach place is because it gets me back into nature.

Meditation

Meditation is new to me, but it's becoming an increasingly important addition to my life. It feels good to quiet myself, be in the here and now, and not worry about what happened yesterday or will happen tomorrow. Old perfectionist me often feels I'm not doing a good enough job, not meditating "right." But staying with it delivers many benefits. I experience such a sense of gratitude for all I have. When I stop stewing over what's wrong, I'm able to see my virtues more than my faults. I feel better about myself. Slowly, but surely, I hope this meditative focus will help me be less judgmental and more accepting of myself and the people and events in my life.

Meditation also helps me get rid of the shoulds and oughts and the why-don't-yous that have made me feel inadequate for so long. Now I find I'm not paying as much attention to these outside-inside voices that ask if I really should be taking a nap or listening to a book when I haven't washed my dishes or gotten my desk organized. Is it okay to feel so self-satisfied? I'm surprised I can answer without hesitation, "Of course, it is!"

Writing

Maybe most important to me now is to keep on writing. Even though I can't actually write the way I was used to, I'm still filled with ideas I want to write about. How to do it? My answer appeared when Judith came into my life as described earlier. Creating this book, with its many collaborative editing sessions, has been hard work and fun, and it has made my life feel whole. Apparently, I still need to feel productive to find that wholeness. And even while we were finishing this book, I was seething with ideas for another book I wanted to begin.

— *Stuff* —

Not only have I been slowing down, I've also been downsizing. Getting rid of stuff is one of the hardest jobs we oldsters face. But for me it's also brought unexpected benefits.

I've now downsized for the third (and presumably last) time. Going from a large, two-story Tudor brick home in a residential neighborhood to a five-room, two-bath condo was the first. The last was to two rooms in a retirement residence with a small closet, two cupboards, and no study. How I agonized each time: "How in the world am I going to accommodate all the stuff I consider essential to my life? And how am I going to get rid of the rest?"

I vividly remember standing in the middle of my condo when I was packing up for the last time, looking at the endless things I had to decide what to do with: What should go to charity, what to the thrift store, what to the family (close to downsizing themselves)? The pile of what to take with me seemed like a little pile compared to the others. Boy, was I glad I had help from the woman in our church who guides people through these kinds of decisions. But even with her help, it wasn't easy.

Where Did It All Go?

One of the first decisions had to be to get rid of my computer, which meant living without word processing, the Web, and e-mail! But that was easier than it might have been, because I'd already been giving up one part after another as my vision deteriorated. So, I gave it away. That is, I tried, but it turned out I actually had to pay for the salvage people to take it, even though we delivered it to their very door.

Next came the remains of my professional library. Even though I would no longer be able to read any of it, it was a terrible wrench to consign most of it to the recycle bin. I must admit I did keep a dozen or so of "the classics."

The file cabinets and desk chairs and all they represented were next to go. I kept a big old red library table fitted out as a desk, a two-drawer file cabinet, and one bookcase. They now constitute my study under the window along the wall of my bedroom.

What would I do with all my sets of dishes and wineglasses, things I'd held onto through the previous moves? I'd loved setting lovely tables for guests. But there wasn't room for all this fancy paraphernalia in the two drawers and two cabinets in my miniature kitchen. (Nor was there room for the guests.) Let's not forget—I'd moved into a retirement home because I'd become so high risk in the kitchen and shouldn't be cooking.

Most of these relics from the past I gave away to agencies who could raise money by reselling them. Now the little entertaining I do is in a restaurant or the very nice dining room in my retirement center.

I'm still hanging on to some of the carefully wrapped and packed-away sentimental bric-a-brac in my storage space downstairs. Every once in a while I take some of the things out and then carefully rewrap them and put them away again. I imagine some day I'll be able to let most of them go, but I'm not ready yet. They still have a place in my heart. Maybe some of these will end up in my children's homes. But I'm not counting on it. After all, all three of them are in their sixties and themselves on the verge of downsizing. Maybe I'll have a Crone bric-a-brac sale someday.

In the past I've had fun giving away baskets and other treasures to people who've admired them—like my wood burl from my friend Florence. It didn't have value to anyone but me, but it brought back her face when I looked at it. I didn't want to give it away, and I didn't want to leave it for others to deal with. Judith admired it many times, and when I moved, I gave it to her. This solution gave both of us pleasure.

Pondering

The last move required parting with what had seemed like essentials. Though this paring down was hard at the time, it's such a relief now! So much of what seemed precious turned out to be excess baggage. I no longer need this stuff to show me who I am and how good I am.

With my vision so limited, I used to be in a constant state of hunting for things. Now I have just what I need, and there are only a few places to look for them. While I still manage to misplace things, having less has really made daily living easier.

I continue to wonder why I don't miss the opera and ballet, my precious books and dishes, and committees that were so important at the time. Rather than feeling deprived, I find I'm actually relieved. My reduced energy and vision and hearing loss have made many of these activities and possessions burdensome or frustrating. Less clutter of all kinds has opened space and time for me to fully appreciate what I choose to have in my life now. And I'm finding joy behind the new doors that have opened, offering me a simpler, less demanding life, allowing me to find satisfaction in just being.

Chapter Ten

Staying Connected

What would I do without my family and friends?

This is what I ask myself every time my children come to organize my finances, take me shopping, or help me find something I've misplaced. It's what I ask when a longtime friend comes regularly to dole out my medications, when a more recent friend comes weekly to read poetry, when a small church group gathers for discussion at my place twice a month.

These people, along with many others, are mainstays of my quality old age. How could I do without the loving support of each of these relationships?

— *Family* —

I don't have to look further than my three children to see that each relationship is unique in its own way.

In my mind's eye, Melody, at four, is flying down the sidewalk on her brand-new tricycle, laughing and obviously exhilarated by racing into the wind. I don't think she's slowed down since. I see Craig as a twenty-month-old, still in diapers, squatting and watching with total absorption as a ladybug crawls up a blade of grass. To this day his intense passion for nature is a major part of his makeup. And I remember Dale, even as a three-year-old, looking up into my face and asking, "You okay, Mommy?" Then he patted my knee when I assured him I was. He's never lost his empathy, his compassion for others.

Now my grandchildren and great-grandchild have been enlivening this old age of mine with their own takes on life. Milo is that great-grandchild. At four, as you might imagine, he's the perfect child—precocious, fun, and everything a great-grandmother could want.

I've also been blessed with a big, extended family, which seems to always remember Aunt Eileen and include her in family doings. I bask in the affection and support of both the immediate and extended family. The picnics, the weddings, and the get-togethers keep me involved with four generations. I identify with these kinfolk, feel at home with them, keep growing in my old age because of them.

A Different Way of Listening

Family dynamics change. My desire to do more listening and less talking surely applies here. It no longer seems so important for me to hold forth about my affairs and beliefs. I'm truly interested in all that's going on with the people in all the generations of my family. I want to listen in a way that helps us learn from each other and understand each other better.

I'm trying to listen for clues that will let me know if the younger folks want advice or if they just want to share their lives with someone who loves them and won't be judgmental. Just because I've got all this so-called wisdom stored away in my aged brain doesn't mean I have to spill it. I constantly caution myself, "Don't be so free with your unsolicited advice. Wait until you're asked." And, thank goodness, I'm able to realize how much they have to offer me.

Rituals

Another shift for me is realizing and accepting that family rituals won't necessarily be passed on, as I used to think they would be. I didn't have rituals as a child with my single mom. As a consequence, I worked hard to establish them when I had my own family. But now my children are putting more emphasis on the traditions they're developing in their own families. Imagine one or the other of them whisking my grandchildren away for skiing instead of going to our traditional Christmas gathering! My first reaction when this started happening was that they were being selfish. But I didn't have to look far to see that I was the selfish one. It doesn't work to hold onto rituals because of the meaning they have for us old folks.

I know that I'll never be alone on Mother's Day, Thanksgiving, or Christmas, even if the rituals change. What's more, I'm getting to the place where I can say that whenever we're together as a family, it will be a celebration. It doesn't need to be on The Day and doesn't have to fit my previous definition of how things were to be done.

By changing my expectations, I'm even finding new rituals as satisfying as the large family gatherings of old. Now my youngest son and I enjoy preparing the Christmas turkey, dressing, and gravy ingredients at his home the day before the family gathers there. We get it ready to put into the oven the next morning for all who are expected for dinner. How I look forward to the fun we have, just the two of us in the quiet preholiday kitchen. I notice that anticipating the pleasure of these family times adds greatly to my enjoyment of this stage of life.

It's Not Just About Holidays

My older son was diagnosed with prostate cancer just before his sixtieth birthday. I was beside myself with worry and wondered how I could be anything but a wet blanket at his birthday party. I hit upon the idea that I would tell stories about him as an adorable child, and this lifted me out of my despair.

As it turned out, I needn't have worried about my participation. He and his wife decided to celebrate his birthday quietly with a couple who were longtime friends. My first reaction was to feel hurt that I wasn't included. I think if he hadn't been so ill I might have had a harder time letting go of my own disappointment. As it was, it took a while, but I realized the focus had to be on what he needed, not on me.

But what about when more of the focus needs to be on me, when I need increasing help as I get even deeper into old age? I can't take for granted that my children will be able to provide it. They have their own full lives. I resolved years ago not to be a burdensome parent, putting out tentacles to hold them. And it's truly important to me for them to have time to enjoy their grandchildren, their retirement, or whatever comes along. Not that I don't hope they'll show up on Mother's Day with a fistful of flowers if I'm out of commission!

— *Friends* —

Family is important. So are friends. Friends provide yet another way to share thoughts, feelings, and experiences. Being with them makes everything from sipping tea at home to going to the ballet more fun. They provide acceptance and understanding, a place to turn to in good times and bad. Almost every friend I've had has helped me explore a new part of myself.

When we were raising our children together, Betty saw in me an intellectual bent I'd never recognized. She managed to get me to my first university class—peasant embroidery, of all things! Mae unknowingly helped me learn to be funny. She provided the model in her own contagious sense of humor. Bruce, in love with poetry himself, said, "Of course you can learn poetry; you talk like a poet"—a revelation to me. Florence, my department head, was a combination of mentor and close friend. She helped me see my potential by reflecting back to me things I said or did that showed skill or insight.

Making and Losing Friends

We need to be able to make new friends at any time of life. From the times I've been put in the position of needing to do this, it's become clear that it makes a difference how I approach people. If I'm open and accepting, I'm likely to be met with more openness and acceptance.

Though I hadn't always approached people with the intention of talking to them, now I talk to people. Initiating common, everyday pleasantries—with a smile, a cheery greeting, a small compliment—more often than not opens the way for a conversation and even a friendship. It's worth risking a rebuff.

Sometimes we lose friends through falling out or drifting apart. One thing I've learned from the painful times when this has happened is that I must not blame myself for everything that goes wrong. Even more importantly: I cannot blame others. I have to realize that times and circumstances change. There has to be a good balance between looking honestly at my own role in what's happened and trying to understand how the other person is perceiving the same situation.

Being My Own Friend

More and more I'm aware of the importance of being friends with myself. As David Whyte says in his poem "At Home," "So, I am here with no company but my house, my garden and my well-peopled solitude."

Not that I'm a loner, but I do enjoy my own company. When I take my daily walk, I love to go at my own pace, think my own thoughts, stop when I want to feel the bark of a tree or pick up a leaf. These are things I probably wouldn't do if I were walking and chatting with a friend.

I find it so satisfying to have my apartment to myself. Then I can spout poetry whenever I feel like it, be tidy or not, listen to my own needs and preferences. Do I want the radio or TV on or off? Do I want to have a friend over?

Time to myself is something I cherish, but even then my life is richer because of my friends. I turn to them in my memory and relive all the good times we've had together. And they sometimes pop up more tangibly. A dear friend called one evening from miles away to describe to me the moonrise she was watching, because she knew I'd love to share that with her.

— *Community* —

Community activities offer another level of connection. They give a sense of purpose, broadened contacts and perspectives, a sense of belonging where I'm known and valued, and a way to work with others on things we all care about.

Throughout my life, I've found community in many different places: in my neighborhood, my profession, my church, and volunteer activities.

As a young mother, I found it in my children's PTAs, the local library, and the coop schools. As an adult student in the academic community, I found it in the classroom and lab. As a teacher and researcher, I found it working with colleagues, students, families, and children. I continue to glow over what my colleagues and I did together.

Even more, I rejoice in what my former students have gone on to do. One has now retired after twenty-five years as the head of an international association of private schools. Another is the head of child development at a major university. One was invited to the White House by

First Lady Hillary Clinton to present her research on early language development.

Connections at This Stage

Since I retired, I've had the good fortune and good sense to get involved in some pretty good organizations. These connections offer me continued learning, support, and companionship for making this old age of mine so fulfilling.

My church is a mainstay—social, intellectual, and spiritual. There I can work with like-minded people on issues important to me, such as social justice, environmental protection, and human rights. The classes I've taken and groups I've been part of have changed the way I look at myself and the possibilities for living a good life.

Our Unitarian-Universalist church has what we call covenant groups. These provide a way to feel like an integral part of the whole through interaction with a few people in an intimate setting. The nine people in my group feel almost like family. We talk and listen and offer support to each other. It's a comfort to know and be known so well.

Another organization that's opened up new dimensions for me is Crone. Though I've never embraced the ideal of perpetual youth, it took Crone to show me how to put real value on aging itself. I'd started in my sixties to plan for a good old age, but in Crone, during my seventies, I found like-minded women to support that intention and to offer ideas through workshops, conversation groups, and the newsletter.

Crone has helped me find a new way of experiencing friendship. I'd never realized how important an all-female group could be. In fact, I'd sometimes even scoffed at going out with women. In Crone I've found it's loads of fun, and I revel in the many friends I've made there and the things we do together.

It's not that I don't welcome male friends into my life. I do. They are special to me in different ways. It's lovely to be taken out to dinner occasionally. And, maybe it's a throwback to an earlier time, but I appreciate it when gallant gentlemen friends compliment me, banter with me, and ask how they can help.

Retirement Community

Now I'm living in the community at the Hearthstone. Here it's easy to encounter a diversity of people—at meals and birthday and holiday gatherings, in the laundry room or the elevator. We chuckle over everyday happenings (not gossip, of course) or discuss meatier issues. Many social activities are available to residents, and I participate in a few: a writing group, lectures and concerts, and occasional trips. I'm so pleased to know I will not have to move again, make another set of new friends, or adjust to a new community. I'm here to stay.

Pondering

Our relationships with people change as we go through the stages of life, especially during the later stages. Parent-child roles often reverse, friendships wax and wane, the student becomes the mentor. And the ways we fit into groups also change. We have to accept each change. Then, sometimes integrating the changes into our lives seems like a balancing act.

Talk about parent-child role reversals. I used to remind my children to wipe their noses; now they have to remind me to wipe mine, which all too often I don't realize is dripping. I'm so grateful they're willing to do this, and I can accept it. And I'm grateful for the grandchildren and great-grandchild they've provided. Now I can revel in my role as matriarch, dispensing wisdom to all who gather at my knee.

As for friendships, I find I especially treasure a friendship that has never waned over more than fifty years. Elaine and I raised our children together, and now they're all senior citizens! Our sons, both in their sixties, faced life-threatening illnesses at the same time. The fact that Elaine and I could share our sadness and anxiety made the crisis more tolerable for both of us.

This is the kind of support we can still offer each other. Having such a long-term friend just a telephone call away adds immeasurably to my well-being as well as to hers. It's also such a comfort to share our increasing losses, especially of longtime mutual friends. It's good to remember, to chuckle over an event of fifty years ago involving someone we've known for so long and who will no longer be part of our lives.

I also rejoice in the waxing friendships with young people, who bring spontaneity, a breath of fresh air, and hope and vision. It's especially meaningful to me when they tell me they love having me as a friend, that our friendship brings them a whole new way to look at life.

My former student Anne gradually became my mentor. Years ago, I helped her get her first book published. Later, she was the one who helped me with the increasingly high-tech requirements of modern publishing.

How has my community involvement changed? Retirement brought a myriad of changes. As I contemplated it, I felt threatened. I wondered where my sense of self would come from when I gave up my professional status. I needn't have worried. I've found that's not what gives me my sense of self. It's there in almost everything I involve myself in. Here's just one example. In Crone, leadership and management roles have given me the old sense of being a contributor, of being a worthwhile person.

My children, my friends, and my broader community continue to be sources of learning, caring, and affirmation that shape me in my old age. Nurturing and being nurtured are even more important now than ever, as are both time alone and time with family and friends. I feel such gratitude to all those who weave their diverse lives with mine to make such a rich, vintage tapestry.

Chapter Eleven

Taking Stock

I Like Being Old is the story of my journey into a joyful and fulfilling old age.

It's not that I haven't made mistakes. But the successes, the mistakes, and even the routine have all been part of the mix. And, I'm happy to say, in this taking stock I've come to believe I've basically done a good job—in my marriage, my parenting, my profession, and now my retirement years. Isn't that a good thing to be able to say at ninety?

Take note that I won't be retiring to a rocking chair! Anticipation makes life worth living, especially in old age. I look forward to each tomorrow, as many as there may be, and continue to plan for the future.

Making a Dream Come True

This brings me to my recent trip to the Grand Canyon, a lifelong dream. I had long felt it was almost un-American to miss one of the great wonders of the world, which was less than three hours away by air, with no passport needed. This trip had kept its appeal while many other dreams seemed like so much busyness in the scheme of elder life I now find so rewarding.

People asked me if it would be worth the effort, since I wouldn't be able to actually see the grandeur. I replied with the old adage "Half a loaf is better than none."

So I went, accompanied by my younger son, who was near retirement himself. True, I saw most of the color and contour through his word pictures. But the grandeur was seeping into my being as we stood at the various viewpoints. I felt I truly experienced the magnificence of that vast and wondrous miracle created by nature's winds and waves.

Not only did we go to the Grand Canyon, but we extended our trip to the incredible red rock country around Sedona, Arizona. This was complete with a helicopter trip that took us down among the massive red rock formations, canyons, and caves, where many Indian peoples made their homes through the ages.

This trip was so fulfilling. I have such a sense of gratitude that I could experience the grandeur in the company of my son, who made it all work. I'm grateful I followed this dream when I did. After all, I don't know when time will run out.

I'd love to stick around for as long as I feel good about myself, as long as my children are still glad I'm alive, as long as my friends like being with me. What a joy to wake up each morning, see the sky—blue or gray—and look forward to all the good things that will happen, like maybe walking around the lake.

End-of-Life Planning

It's obvious I'm in no hurry to die, but I don't fear death. True, at ninety I do think more often about this last major event of my life and wonder what it will be like, this dying. These aren't morbid thoughts, just looking ahead.

What I do fear, like so many of us do, is a long illness that would rob me of the joy and dignity that have made me feel good about my old age so far. I know I can't say for sure how I'll react if I do become ill, but there are some things I can be putting in place now to make it easier to cope.

For one thing, I've already laid out my wishes on end-of-life issues. I've stated clearly I don't want to be kept alive just for the sake of being kept alive. I've tended to the legal things, like power of attorney and physicians' directives. I've talked with my family to make sure they understand what I want, so they're all on board if, for example, I choose to stop eating if I feel I'm just waiting to die.

These arrangements are critical, but equally important are attitudes I've developed as I've aged, and as I've learned to cope with increasing disabilities. I'll need to hold to my belief that I am the creator of my own happiness and well-being. I'll need to continue to accept change as inevitable and stay open to new possibilities. I truly believe that these attitudes can help me continue to create a good life, and the best proof will be that I can apply them if I have to face a long illness.

A debilitating illness will in no way diminish the good life I've had. If I'm no longer able to keep doing the things I want to do, all my rich store of life experiences will still be there to appreciate and relive.

So Many Things to Think About

What about legacy? I tell myself I'm not concerned about such things, but is that really true? I don't expect my work to live on. My books definitely aren't going to have the longevity of Homer's Iliad. But the work I did with colleagues and students started ripples that are ever widening. I'm proud of this professional legacy.

I've had a lifelong love affair with nature. My children tell me they inherited their own love of nature as a gift from their father and me. It started when they were very young, with family tent camping in the forest, mostly under primitive conditions. They've all become conservationists in their own ways, and the work they've chosen to do has served the earth. I'm surely proud of that legacy.

My friends keep telling me the way I'm aging has influenced them. They say I should write down how I've managed to do so well. This book, I hope, will be my legacy to them and a wider audience.

Do I have regrets? There have been difficult times and everyday frustrations and uncertainties. However, they've made me who I am just as much as the good times have. There's no such thing as a life without ups and downs. I'm convinced I wouldn't be as happy or as good a human being as I am without all the mistakes and disappointments as well as the joys and successes.

There are things I wish I could change, one being the too-high expectations I held for my children. Firstborns generally bear the brunt of inexperienced parenting, and mine certainly did. By the time my third came along, I was much more relaxed. But, on the other hand, all three have become productive, worthy adults. There must have been enough good parenting to outweigh the mistakes.

Would I want to be young again? I've never bought into the idea I wanted to be young again so I could do it right. I have the idea I might not make the same mistakes, but I might make others even more devastating. There's much to be learned from the errors we make and much satisfaction from righting them. No, indeed, I wouldn't want to be young again. I'm glad to be through with the insecure teenage agony, the lean years raising a young family, and the midlife upheavals.

I Started Years Ago

One of the things I notice as I look back is that I've been preparing for positive adjustment to my old age for many years. For example, as I said in Chapter Four, I made the decision in my early sixties to take responsibility for my own happiness. The practice of being happy has done more than anything else to give me the attitudes I depend on today.

Noted developmental psychologist Erik Erikson provided me with motivation when I encountered his theories on the stages of life in my early years of teaching human development. He said old age is a time when people reflect on their lives and accomplishments and begin to prepare for death. If they feel good about how they lived their lives, they tend to accept death. If they feel their lives were meaningless and they had many unfulfilled goals, they tend to fear death.

I see now that I started back then, without being aware of it, to learn how to end up in the group of elders who feel good about themselves. Along with becoming less critical of myself, I gradually began to recognize that what I was doing was worthwhile and to have a greater belief in myself. I slowly absorbed how important it was for me, both personally and professionally, to keep learning and to stay open to new challenges and opportunities. Somehow, these shifts allowed me to try things I might otherwise not have tried and made me less afraid of making mistakes.

Reaching Out

These shifts are also helping me reach out more at a time when many old people shut themselves off. I don't want to scare people off with a stern and forbidding face. I want to invite interactions with those I meet, with my head up and with a pleasant face. I'm actually more outgoing because of the successes I've had in being open.

For example, a young man saw me resting on my favorite bench during a walk. When I smiled at him, he stopped to tell me he wished he had his brushes and paints, saying, "You make such a lovely picture sitting there."

When I responded with genuine incredulity, "I do?" he described my dusty pink and soft purple outfit against the background with foxglove flowers of the same colors. I was surprised and pleased to find that even at this advanced age I was being viewed approvingly.

Some Surprises

Some of what seems important to me now surprises me; my perspective has changed.

I used to see things having to do with spirituality as not my thing. Then, a few years ago, I took a class at my church called "Building Your Own Theology." The culminating activity for this eight-week course was for each class member to create his or her own credo: "What I Believe."

I came up with several beliefs that have been significant contributors to my good old age. Here are some examples:

- Life is a gift and a giver of gifts to be treasured and rejoiced in each day.
- Life is impartial, neither singling me out for special favors nor to be a victim.
- Being happy acknowledges the gifts of this world, and living happy is up to me.

My credo didn't include discussion of an afterlife. It's not that I deny that such a phenomenon may exist, but the good life I've lived and am living is what I want to celebrate. In the credo I did identify my belief in a transcendental life force and in the necessity of both community and solitude.

Recognizing the value of solitude is part of what led me to the meditation I took up several years ago. Though I consider myself a novice, I notice that I feel better all day when I meditate for thirty or forty minutes in the morning. I feel certain that this practice has helped me to detach myself from perceived problems and given me a greater acceptance of what is.

Loved Ones Show the Way

My credo and meditation have helped me to face the idea of death with little anxiety. My experiences with the deaths of loved ones have also contributed to the way I face the prospect of my own death.

Helen, a friend from Crone, was diagnosed with cancer and knew she had only a few months to live. A group of friends offered her daily support—helping with physical needs, being there to talk or be silent with her. Helen gave this group, and the wider community, a real gift in the way she chose to conduct her dying. She was open about her own fears and feelings and gave others the chance to explore them, and their own, with her. Though I couldn't be a part of that support group, and was able to visit her only once, I felt inspired by Helen's grace and generosity in her last days.

Then there was Roy, my husband of fifty-four years. During a yearlong battle with cancer, he was in and out of the hospital, with several surgeries. The regard he had for all of us who were loving and caring for him was an inspiration. Right up until he died, he was an uncomplaining patient.

When we knew the end was near, he decided with his doctor and me that it was time to be taken off life support. That evening, I was sitting with him, holding his hand. He turned and whispered, "Aren't I going to have a birthday pretty soon?"

I said, "You sure are. You're going to be eighty-two a week from today."

We were quiet for a few moments, and I said, "It sounds to me like you might like to stay around for your birthday." He nodded yes. And so our children and I quickly got up a little party in his hospital room on his birthday. We invited our closest friends and family and smuggled our cat up the back stairway in a covered basket. We kept it short. Roy couldn't participate much, but it was obvious he loved every minute of his last birthday celebration. That night they began removing life support.

Perhaps even more important for the children and me was the time we spent with him just after his death a week later. With the help of the nurses, we removed the medical paraphernalia and reduced the floral offerings to a few. We turned down the lights and lit candles. We played his favorite Segovia guitar music and sat around the bed crying and laughing and telling family stories starring Dad. It was a joyous time, in spite of the deep sadness we were feeling. We had such a sense of relief that his yearlong ordeal was finally at an end. When we looked at his peaceful face, it seemed to us he was also glad he could go.

Now that's the kind of send-off I'd like!

Pondering

From Roy's death I learned that the best way to ensure good care is to be thoughtful of others and to accept help without making caregivers miserable. I learned a powerful lesson from the patience and consideration that this man, often impatient in earlier years, showed with all of us who cared for him. His gratitude seemed boundless.

Helen's openness about her dying is one of the reasons I'm as open to talking about death as I am now. From another Crone friend, Jean, I learned the dignity in choosing to reject medical treatment just to prolong her life. From all three I also learned acceptance. There was no "why me?" in any of them. I hope the attitudes and practices I've developed for coping with my old age will see me through with Roy's, Helen's, and Jean's grace, whatever the very end of life brings to me.

At this stage of my life, I live with the certainty of death and the uncertainty of not knowing when death will come. But this doesn't cast a shadow over living, over my joy and anticipation of what's to come. I savor what each day brings in a different way than I used to. I enjoy taking more time and paying attention to the little details. I'm discovering a new appreciation for things I never even considered interesting before, like poetry and meditation. These are just the latest in a lifelong series of changes that have led me to this state—so in love with life, still looking forward, but willing to let go when the time comes.

Acknowledgments

Our deepest thanks to Sidney and Harlan Roedel for their careful reading and editing and excellent suggestions for making this a better book, and for their support in so many ways. Thanks also to Dale Allen and Peter Greenfield, who gave us valuable suggestions on the whole book, and to Rita Bresnahan, Mary Casey, Ann Gordon, and Miriam Reed for reading and making suggestions on individual chapters.

Author biographies

K. Eileen Allen

Eileen began to focus on lifespan development after nearly 50 years as a child development specialist in university settings. As she herself aged, Eileen began seeing the parallels between early childhood and old age. Even before she retired, she advocated for the elderly in 1981- 82 in Washington, D.C. As a Congressional Science Fellow, she was involved with the Select Committee on Aging, under the venerable Rep. Claude Pepper.

Long years before, she started her career as a cooperative parent in her son's preschool in Seattle in 1950. This humble beginning led to years as an undergraduate at night to get her bachelors and masters degrees while raising her three children. Next came a faculty position at the University of Washington, and 16 years later, one at the University of Kansas. She published many research papers and is the author of seven early childhood textbooks, two of which are now in their sixth and seventh editions.

Eileen retired in 1987, and she and her husband returned to Seattle. For several years she continued to publish and consult, including with the team at Microsoft designing hardware and software for children two-to-five. She has now shifted her writing to the field of aging.

Judith Starbuck

Judith learned interviewing and editing skills helpful in working with Eileen on this book as a journalism student at Kent State University (in Ohio). Since graduation in 1964, she has written, done layout, and served as editor for the publications of several non-profit organizations.

At age 55 she started volunteering on Crone of Puget Sound's newsletter. It was there she met Eileen and their friendship blossomed. Judith's mother is the same age as Eileen and, like Eileen, is a role model for positive aging into the 90s.

Judith has worked with neighbors in her local community for the past 15 years to return the heavily overgrown wooded area in a nearby park to a sustainable urban forest. She is currently writing a history of this restoration effort. She and her husband have lived in the same house in Seattle for 40 years.